SALADOLOGY

Food memories have shaped the way we cook at home and the food we serve in our restaurants – big flavours always with fresh ingredients, served simply, seasoned generously with lots of imagination. Perhaps this isn't your typical salad cookbook. It claims no great secrets to wellness. We're just passionate guys who have eaten just about everything and are in constant search for the most delicious food: things that stop us in our tracks and make us go 'wow!'.

The last drops of vinaigrette mopped up from a simple tomato salad, a perfect little pintxo in a Spanish tapas bar, or a mouth-burning, tongue-numbing authentic kung pao; the best food has a strange addiction that keeps on pulling you back for more. *Saladology* is about reimagining what a salad can be – simple or more complex, light or indulgent; there are no rules, but an emphasis on delicious. This book is a journal, in a way, a collection of salads and ideas inspired by our favourite food experiences, turned into something we hope you'll really enjoy too.

& LOCAL
SPROUT & CO
KITCHEN
HEALTHY, SEASONAL & LOCAL
CHARRED CHICKEN TACO
MIDDLE EASTERN CHICKEN
SIGNATURE SALADS

SPR☉UT & CO

SALADOLOGY

Fresh ideas for delicious salads

THEO KIRWAN

MITCHELL BEAZLEY

CONTENTS

THE SPROUT BROTHERS

Jack on Theo

Theo and I are the youngest of seven siblings. We naturally shared lots of things growing up, including a bedroom until our teens.

In a family so large it's always a fight for attention. Theo often insisted on making a speech before dinner, standing on his chair so we could all hear his views as a five-year-old. It was a sign of things to come, as when he finished school, he went off to study acting.

Food was often at the centre of our relationship. We took over family cooking duties by the time we were tall enough to work a hob. Mum was brilliant as she would push us to try things and then just let us at it. On special occasions we'd visit the market together and pick out exotic produce we had no idea how to cook. We bonded over cooking, but I don't think either of us dreamt we'd start Sprout together.

Building a business with anyone is hard and testing, but doing it with someone that I admire, respect and love is special.

In Sprout, Theo has combined his two big passions, cooking and entertaining. Eating with him is always a surprise. Flavours that I would never dream of are put together. His vision for what might work is often so far ahead of how the rest of us are thinking. It's inspiring to be around him when he's creating.

It's obvious he has a flair for being in front of a camera, but few probably realize the time and dedication he puts into the recipe videos he creates. He goes all in.

I probably kicked off the cooking bug between us, but now that he has written our first cookbook, it's time for me to admit, my younger brother is better at cooking than me!

Theo on Jack

I owe my brother a lot for helping me throughout my life and Firstly, for allowing me the space to write this book while he remained focussed on our business. And secondly, for giving me a job in the juice bar all those years ago.

I probably wouldn't have discovered my passion for food if it were not for Jack. As the head chef in our house growing up, he would draft me in as his inexperienced commis to prep the mundane tasks. We used to joke saying, 'Jack does the cookin', I do the choppin'' when we were kids. Ironically, now I do the choppin' and the cookin' most of the time.

From an early age Jack had a love of food, and knew he wanted to get into the business. After a stint in Avoca, developing products and working in the kitchen, his then boss and our cousin, Simon, saw his obvious potential and offered him a space to open a juice bar concession within Avoca at just 23 years old. Sprout & Co was born.

My brother and I are very different, but we have a consistent common interest: we both love eating – a lot. Throughout our life we've bonded over, well, over-spending on food. Where I struggle with decision-making and procrastination in daily life, Jack makes things happen, always has a vision for the big picture, pushing things on, constantly eyeing the next opportunity, and amazing me and our team with exciting plans for the future. An inspiring leader, and a natural delegator (like getting me to do his choppin'), he gets the best out of people.

OUR STORY

The idea for Sprout & Co started when Jack cooked with a freshly picked, ripened tomato at the Ballymaloe Cookery School and couldn't believe the difference in flavour between it and what you find at your supermarket. It was the lightbulb moment that made us think about how a business could be built around just that: fresh in-season produce, grown locally.

We started out making cold-pressed juice, but our dream was a restaurant, and at the end of 2015, we got the keys to our first on Dublin's Dawson Street. People told us a restaurant would never work at that location, as the previous three tenants had all struggled to succeed. We ploughed ahead anyway!

From day one we chose not to take the easy path. We made everything from scratch – dressings, sauces and dips were prepared daily.

Break-of-dawn vegetable deliveries came in from Dublin's Smithfield Market, and out of our broom-closet-sized kitchen came tray upon tray of whole roasted chickens shredded by hand ahead of lunch service.

In the first week, as we opened our doors, to our genuine surprise we had queues forming out of the restaurant and up the street. What followed was a whirlwind as we tried to figure out how to make it all work.

Since then, with the help of our team, we've gone on to open many restaurants across Ireland. What started out as a niche way of approaching food is fast becoming the way many people are choosing to eat.

In 2018 we became farmers

Tasting a salad leaf pulled directly from the soil is a reminder of what a salad leaf should taste like and why growing organically on our own farm was a mad idea worth pursuing.

'Food tastes better when you know where it's come from' has always been our philosophy. So growing for ourselves on Sprout Farm meant we could be involved in every step of the journey towards our customer's bowl – a genuine field-to-fork story, from sowing the seeds, pulling weeds, harvesting and delivering direct to our restaurants for our team of chefs to prepare.

Our head farmer, Trevor Harris, a passionate and inspiring biodynamic grower, oversees everything. We are incredibly proud and fortunate to work with someone so knowledgeable and dedicated to his farming principles.

We've tried our hand at just about every vegetable variety the Irish climate can produce – tomatoes, beetroots, spring onions, cabbages, cauliflower, sprouting broccoli, courgettes and cucumber to name a few, but now with a little hard-earned wisdom, we're focused on salad leaves, the ingredient we use the most in our restaurants. Throughout the year you'll find lettuces, kale, spinach, tatsoi, mustard greens and rocket growing on the Sprout Farm in County Kildare.

THE LARDER

Welcome to my larder. Here, I've compiled a list of staple ingredients that we use in the restaurants and items that I always keep in stock in my kitchen. Having these products to hand will help you through the recipes in this book. All that's left is picking up the fresh ingredients.

FATS

Olive oil
Use a standard olive oil for all dressings or for cooking, as the flavour is more neutral.

Extra virgin olive oil
Always have a good-quality fruity olive oil to use as a final splash to finish dishes.

Neutral oils
Vegetable and sunflower oil are ideal for flavouring with aromatics to create crispy toppings as well as fragrantly flavoured oil, which you can use to bring unique flavour to the simplest of things, like scrambled egg.

SALT

I love flaky sea salt and I use Maldon in my cooking rather exclusively. However, in this book, we use regular fine salt for cooking and seasoning dressings, and flaky salt to flavour and garnish finished dishes. Use fine salt as a default and flaky salt only when specified.

Mustards
There is always a place in my kitchen for different types of mustard, from Dijon, wholegrain and English (yellow) to the classic American French's, whether to emulsify a dressing or to bring heat to a marinade.

ACID

Vinegars
We use an array of vinegars throughout the book. It's worth investing in good-quality white and red wine vinegars, as they will make a big difference to the flavour of your dressings. All the pickles are made with rice vinegar, my favourite, but can be swapped for apple cider vinegar or white or red wine vinegar.

Citrus
Most of the recipes that feature either lemon or lime juice are then finished with more to serve. We can't test for fruit that has little juice, so it's always good to have extra on the table.

Preserved vegetables
Most of our salad recipes include some sort of preserved vegetable; see pages 200–201 for ideas for making quick pickles.

The following shop-bought products are a quick way to elevate salad dishes and are always good to have in store: capers, cornichons, preserved lemons, kimchi, olives and pickled guindilla hot peppers or pickled sliced jalapeños.

UMAMI

Adding umami is not just a matter of seasoning with salt. This intense savouriness brings depth to most foods. The following are the sources of umami we use throughout the book: soy sauce, fish sauce, white miso paste, gochujang, anchovy fillets in oil and Parmesan cheese. A selection of seasoning sauces that are also worth having are: Worcestershire sauce, oyster sauce, Golden Mountain Seasoning Sauce and Maggi Liquid Seasoning.

SWEETENERS

Most salad dressings require sweetness to bring balance. So I suggest stocking a good local runny honey, maple syrup, palm sugar (for the Thai-style dressings) and agave syrup for a neutral sweetness if you want an alternative to sugar.

OTHER ESSENTIALS

Whole spices
For the best flavour, toast whole spices and then freshly grind.

Aromatics
Using fresh ingredients to bring unique flavour is what we do best! Examples include adding very finely chopped garlic or fresh root ginger to a dressing, a little sliced chilli to bring heat and raw allium such as sliced spring onion or red onion to give a dish that desirable rounded flavour.

Herbs
I always have a selection of herbs in the fridge. They are inexpensive and flavourful. Wash your herbs when you bring them home and then store them covered with a damp cloth or tea towel in an airtight container. That way they will stay fresh in the fridge for much longer.

Note: See pages 196–201 for toppings and crispy things, marinades, dressings and quick pickles that feature most often in our recipes – our signature flavour enhancers, if you will – which you will be directed to from the main recipes.

SIMPLE SALADS THAT MAKE EVERYTHING BETTER

BIG GREEN SALAD

This style of salad is what we grew up eating, often alongside our dad's take on spaghetti carbonara. Fresh crisp Butterhead lettuce and a sharp French vinaigrette – perfect for just about any situation!

Serves 4 as a side

60g (2¼oz) walnuts

3 celery sticks, plus any celery leaves you have

1 Butterhead lettuce, leaves separated

75g (2¾oz) good-quality blue cheese, such as Cashel, crumbled

1 quantity French Dressing (see page 197)

1. Toast the walnuts in a small dry frying pan over a medium heat for 3–4 minutes until lightly golden. Remove from the pan and set aside to cool.

2. Snap off the ends of the celery and pull off any stringy bits from the stalks. Slice into small pieces, along with a few celery leaves if you have them.

3. To assemble, I like to use the celery leaves like herbs, so add them to a salad bowl with the celery. Then add the lettuce leaves, toasted walnuts and blue cheese.

4. Pour over as much of the dressing as you like (I use 5 tablespoons). Serve straight away while it's still fresh, as it won't sit for long once dressed.

LITTLE GEMS WITH SWEET MINT DRESSING

The dressing for this simple green salad comes from an Indian-inspired dish we had on our menu called the Bombay Party Bowl. The dressing tastes rather like a savoury mojito and would work equally well with a piece of grilled white fish or halloumi.

....

Serves 4 as a side

1 tablespoon mixed white and black sesame seeds

½ teaspoon pul biber (Aleppo chilli flakes)

2 Little Gem lettuces or 1 Butterhead lettuce, leaves separated

1 shallot, finely sliced into rounds

salt

For the sweet mint dressing

small handful of fresh coriander (about 15g/½oz)

small handful of mint (about 15g/½oz), leaves picked

2 green chillies

2-cm (¾-inch) piece of fresh root ginger, peeled

1 tablespoon sugar

generous pinch of salt

90ml (6 tablespoons) olive oil

juice of 1 lime

2 tablespoons rice vinegar

1. Blitz all the dressing ingredients together in a blender. Taste and adjust the seasoning if necessary. It should be sweet, minty and a little spicy.

2. Toast the sesame seeds in a small dry frying pan over a medium heat for about 2 minutes until the white sesame seeds are lightly golden. Remove from the pan and set aside to cool, then stir in the pul biber with a pinch of salt.

3. To assemble, dress the lettuce leaves in the sweet mint dressing and top with the shallot and toasted sesame seeds and pul biber. Serve immediately.

CHICORY SALAD
WITH MUSTARDY WALNUT & GOUDA 'SALSA'

You can use whatever hard, salty cheese you like here, from Manchego to Cheddar. I particularly love Coolea, a sensational cow's milk Gouda-like cheese from West Cork. This recipe would work equally well as a side salad, starter or even a canapé using the chicory leaves as little tacos.

Serves 4 as a side

2 heads of chicory, leaves separated

100g (3½oz) walnuts

100g (3½oz) Gouda cheese,
or any other hard, salty cheese
you like, cut into small cubes

flaky sea salt

freshly ground black pepper

For the dressing

finely grated zest of 1 orange and
juice of ½

juice of ½ lemon

1 tablespoon Dijon mustard

2 tablespoons extra virgin olive oil,
plus extra to finish

1 tablespoon white wine vinegar

1. Arrange the chicory leaves on a serving platter.

2. Toast the walnuts in a dry frying pan over a medium heat for 3–4 minutes until lightly golden. Remove from the pan and set aside to cool, then roughly chop.

3. To make the dressing, add the orange zest to a bowl, followed by the orange and lemon juice, then mix in the mustard, extra virgin olive oil, vinegar and a pinch of flaky salt along with pepper to taste.

4. Add the cheese cubes and toasted walnuts to the dressing and toss together so that they are all evenly coated.

5. Spoon the cheese and walnuts over the chicory and add a pinch of flaky salt, a good grinding of black pepper and an extra drizzle of extra virgin olive oil.

A SWEET 'JAMMY' RED PEPPER SALAD

The truth is that food is so simple and adaptable, and often the most basic of ingredients can be transformed into so much more. Here, red onions and Romano peppers are sautéed together until jammy and saucy to make a simple midweek salad worthy of serving to an adoring lover. But these peppers can be taken in many other directions – stirred through pasta, spooned over rice or even used as a base for a Spanish tortilla.

Serves 4 as a side

3 tablespoons olive oil

2 red onions, halved and finely sliced into half-moons

2 red Romano peppers, cored, deseeded and sliced into rounds 1cm (½ inch) thick

large handful of basil leaves

large handful of rocket

salt and freshly ground black pepper

For the balsamic dressing

2 tablespoons extra virgin olive oil

1 tablespoon balsamic vinegar

1 tablespoon runny honey

1 tablespoon water

1 garlic clove, grated

1. Pour the olive oil into a large frying pan over a medium-low heat, add the onions and peppers and toss to coat in the oil with a good pinch of salt. Fry, stirring regularly, for 15–20 minutes until the onions are caramelized and the peppers are jammy and soft.

2. To make the dressing, mix all the ingredients together in a small bowl along with a pinch of salt and a grind of black pepper.

3. Toss the basil with the rocket, then spread out across the base of a large serving plate and scatter the sautéed onions and peppers on top.

4. Generously pour the dressing across the dish and finish with a big grind of black pepper.

MISO KALE

Kale in its raw state is a great vehicle for a robust dressing. Once massaged it will absorb the dressing, so you can make the dish a little ahead of time before serving. I have used this rich, sweet and umami miso maple mixture in various ways throughout the book, as a marinade and sauce as well as a dressing. Its versatility is its superpower, and it is a great larder standby that won't go off in a hurry. I've kept this salad simple, but you could add to it with fresh green chilli and spring onion.

Serves 4 as a side

1 garlic clove, minced

1 quantity Miso Maple Dressing (see page 199)

200g (7oz) curly kale, stalks removed and leaves finely sliced

½ quantity Pickled Red Cabbage (see page 201)

½ tablespoon white sesame seeds

salt, if required

1. Add the minced garlic to the miso maple dressing and stir through.

2. Add the kale to a large bowl, toss through 4 tablespoons of the dressing and massage together with your hands. You want the kale to be well dressed, so add more if it's looking a little dry. The kale will turn bright green and soften a little after a while.

3. Meanwhile, toast the sesame seeds in a small dry frying pan over a medium heat for about 2 minutes until lightly golden. Remove from the pan and set aside to cool.

4. Taste the kale for seasoning, adding a pinch of salt if required, then arrange it on a serving dish. Drain the pickled cabbage and pile it on top of the kale.

5. To serve, sprinkle with the toasted sesame seeds.

A LITTLE CUCUMBER AND A LOT OF HERB SALAD

You will always find an abundance of herbs in my kitchen. They are an inexpensive way to add unique fresh flavour to any dish (see page 10 for how I store herbs and keep them fresh for longer). This dressing is best made with a good-quality runny tahini.

Serves 2 as a side

1 large cucumber

2 tablespoons mixed white and black sesame seeds

very small handful of the mint, dill and chives reserved from the dressing (see below)

pinch of pul biber (Aleppo chilli flakes)

salt and freshly ground black pepper

For the tahini dressing

60g (2¼oz) mixed herbs, such as mint, chives, dill, parsley and coriander

3 tablespoons extra virgin olive oil

2 tablespoons tahini

1 garlic clove, peeled

juice of ½ lemon (reserve the remaining half for the salad)

1. Cut the cucumber in half lengthways, scoop out the seedy insides with a teaspoon and set aside to use for the dressing. Slice the cucumber into half-moons 1cm (½ inch) thick and add to a bowl with a big pinch of salt.

2. Toast the sesame seeds in a small dry frying pan over a medium heat for about 2 minutes until the white sesame seeds are lightly golden. Remove from the pan and set aside to cool.

3. To make the dressing, pick the leaves from the mint, finely chop the chives, then tear the dill, parsley and coriander. Reserve a small handful of mint, dill and chopped chives, then add the rest of the herbs to a blender or food processor with all the other dressing ingredients, some salt and pepper and the cucumber seeds. Blitz until you have a creamy green dressing, adding a little cold water if it's too thick.

4. Add 3 tablespoons of the dressing to the cucumber and toss together.

5. Dress the reserved herbs in the juice from the remaining lemon half.

6. In a large serving dish, add the tahini-dressed cucumber, followed by a pile of the lemony herbs, then finally the toasted sesame seeds and pul biber. Season with a little more salt and pepper if needed and serve immediately.

TIGER SALAD

I've learned most of what I know about food from cookbooks, the internet, experimenting and travelling. Xi'an Famous Foods in New York had a 'Tiger Salad' on their menu, and enticed by the name, I just had to recreate it. I love the flavour of the fresh celery with the sweet tart dressing, which takes it to a fun new place. The salad cuts through rich umami dishes, so is best served with an oily dish like a kung pao or stir-fried noodles. You can adapt the recipe to use whatever crunchy veg you have. More traditional recipes use crispy dried shrimp, but I've used fried peanuts to add a roasted crunch instead.

Serves 2 as a side

4 celery sticks, plus any celery leaves you have

2 spring onions

1 green chilli

1 banana shallot

1 small bunch of fresh coriander, stems and all

2–3 tablespoons Fried Peanuts & Crispy Lime Leaves (see page 196)

For the sweet soy & sesame dressing

2 tablespoons sunflower oil

2 tablespoons soy sauce

1 tablespoon sesame oil

1 tablespoon rice vinegar

1 tablespoon maple syrup

1 garlic clove, grated

pinch of flaky sea salt

1. Snap off the ends of the celery and pull off any stringy bits from the stalks. Slice the celery into small pieces, and finely slice the spring onions and green chilli diagonally and add to a bowl. Peel, halve and finely slice the shallot lengthways into long strips, then add to the bowl with the other prepped veg.

2. To make the dressing, mix all the ingredients together in a small bowl. Taste and season with more salt if necessary.

3. Toss the prepped veg with the fresh coriander, leaving the stems whole, then pile it all in a serving bowl or on a plate. Pour over the dressing, gently toss together, then top with the fried peanuts and crispy lime leaves.

SWEET PICKLED CUCUMBER & SHALLOT SALAD

I must credit the Ballymaloe Cookery School in County Cork for this, adapted from memory from their Thai-inspired pickled cucumber salad recipe called Arjard. When you simmer the vinegar and sugar mixture, it becomes a little syrupy and acts as a dressing as well as a pickle liquor. It's great with rich sauces or served with other dishes such as The 'Sataysfied' Chicken on page 137.

Serves 2 as a side

150ml (5fl oz) white wine vinegar

150ml (5fl oz) water

3 tablespoons sugar

1 teaspoon salt

1 cucumber

1 shallot, finely sliced into rounds

1 green chilli, finely sliced

1 red chilli, finely sliced

1. Heat the vinegar, water, sugar and salt in a small saucepan over a medium heat and gently simmer for 5 minutes. Remove from the heat and set aside to cool completely.

2. Cut the cucumber in half lengthways, scoop out the seedy insides with a teaspoon and discard, then slice diagonally into 1-cm (½-inch) thick half moons. Place in a bowl with the shallot and chillies.

3. Once the pickle liquor has cooled, pour it over the vegetables and toss so that they are all coated. Set aside to pickle while you prepare your accompanying dish.

A POSH FENNEL & KOHLRABI SALAD

This is an elegant way to serve fennel. Finely shaved, it still has some crunch but in a fresh, cleansing way. Serve alongside a simple piece of cooked fish, under the sun on a summer's day.

Serves 2 as a main, 4 as a side

1 kohlrabi

1 fennel bulb

juice of ½ lemon

1 orange

1 red chilli, finely sliced

large handful of flat leaf parsley, finely chopped

2 tablespoons olive oil

salt and freshly ground black pepper

1. Peel the kohlrabi, then cut it in half lengthways and finely slice into half-moons using a mandolin if you have one. Trim off the stalks, reserving the fronds, and root end of the fennel bulb, then cut into similarly thin slices. Add the kohlrabi and fennel slices to a bowl with the lemon juice and a generous pinch of salt. Finely chop the reserved fennel fronds and set aside.

2. Zest the orange and set the zest aside. Slice off the top and bottom of the orange, then peel the skin off with a sharp serrated knife, removing as much of the white pith as you can. Cut the orange in half lengthways. Squeeze the juice of one half over the fennel and kohlrabi, then slice the other half into segments.

3. Add the orange segments to the bowl along with the red chilli, parsley, olive oil and 4–5 grinds of black pepper.

4. Pile everything on to a serving plate and top with the orange zest, the chopped fennel fronds and a little more black pepper if needed.

LIGHT, FUN & FLAVOURFUL SALADS

TOMATO & TOFU ~ A TWIST ON CAPRESE

This salad takes the principle of the Italian caprese salad, a combination of tart tomatoes and creamy mozzarella, but subbing silken tofu for the cheese and adapting Asian flavours. You can have a lot of fun playing with this concept, which is inspired by one of my favourite cookbooks, *Momofuku*, and there are endless possibilities: think fresh coriander and cashew pesto or crispy tofu instead of croutons for variations on the classic. I've kept this recipe simple, but the key takeaway here is that tomatoes aren't just for Italian classics and can be explored in various ways if you are willing to break some rules. This is perfect for a summery lunch or dinner served alongside a bowl of jasmine rice and some greens.

Serves 2 as a side

250g (9oz) ripe sweet tomatoes – the most delicious you can get

small handful of basil leaves

2 tablespoons white sesame seeds

2 spring onions

250g (9oz) block of firm silken tofu

For the soy & maple dressing

2 tablespoons rapeseed oil

2 tablespoons rice vinegar

2 tablespoons soy sauce

1 tablespoon maple syrup

1 garlic clove, grated

pinch of flaky sea salt, plus extra for sprinkling

1. To make the dressing, mix all the ingredients together in a bowl. Roughly chop the tomatoes into large chunks, then add to the dressing with the basil leaves and set aside for 10 minutes to allow the tomatoes to release their juices and make for the best flavoured dressing.

2. Meanwhile, toast the sesame seeds in a small dry frying pan over a medium heat for about 2 minutes until lightly golden. Remove from the pan and set aside to cool.

3. Very finely slice the spring onions, then place in a bowl of iced water so that they curl up a little and soften in flavour.

4. Cut the tofu into 2-cm (¾-inch) cubes.

5. To assemble, spoon the saucy tomatoes on to a serving platter, then top with the delicate tofu with a sprinkling of flaky salt, followed by the toasted sesame seeds and drained curly spring onions.

PEPPERS & TOFU WITH LIME-BUTTER PINE NUTS

This recipe is best using peppers cooked on a barbecue, as the smoky flavour adds an extra dimension to the overall dish, but I have given a couple of effective alternative methods of charring them here. The sweet mirin and soy dressing in which the peppers are marinated along with the rich, limey buttered pine nuts are the standout elements of this dish, and why shouldn't I put butter in a salad? But if you'd like to make this plant-based, omit the butter and drizzle with tahini instead.

Serves 2 as a main, 4 as a side

4–6 red peppers, ideally Romano

350g (12oz) block of firm silken tofu

50g (1¾oz) pine nuts

2 tablespoons salted butter

finely grated zest and juice of 1 lime

flaky sea salt

For the mirin & soy dressing

2 tablespoons neutral oil, such as vegetable or sunflower oil

1 tablespoon mirin

1 tablespoon soy sauce

1 tablespoon rice vinegar

½ tablespoon maple syrup

1-cm (½-inch) piece of fresh root ginger, peeled and grated

1 garlic clove, very finely chopped or grated

pinch of salt

1. For the charred peppers, place a wire or grill rack over a high gas flame, add the peppers so that they sit directly over the flame and char for 5 minutes, turning every so often using kitchen tongs, until they are evenly blackened and softened in texture. If you don't have a gas flame, simply do the same but in a griddle pan over a high heat.

2. Once the peppers are ready, transfer to a bowl, place a plate over the top to cover completely and set aside to steam for 10 minutes.

3. Meanwhile, mix all the dressing ingredients together in a small bowl.

4. When the peppers have finished steaming, peel off the blackened skins, which should all come off easily. Pull off the tops and remove the seeds, then split the peppers in half lengthways and slice into strips. Put them back in the bowl you steamed them in, add the dressing and set aside to marinate for a few minutes.

5. Cut the tofu into 4 slices, or cubes.

6. Spoon the marinated peppers on to a serving plate and add the tofu slices or cubes to the middle.

7. Toast the pine nuts in a dry frying pan over a medium heat for about 2 minutes until lightly golden. Add the butter and heat over a medium-high heat until it's foaming and begins to brown. Turn off the heat and add the lime juice.

8. Spoon the hot foaming, buttery pine nut mixture over everything, then finish with the lime zest and a good pinch of flaky sea salt over each piece of tofu.

POTATO TARTARE

I couldn't write a salad book without including a potato salad, so this is my twist with a tangy tartare dressing. I love a good tartare sauce, and this would go great with any fish, chip or fish finger sandwich. I pretty much always have a fridge full of capers, cornichons and gherkins because they are ingredients that will immediately elevate your food. It's worth preparing all the garnishes, as it makes the dish visually pleasing as well as adding a crunchy, tart-tasting texture.

Serves 4 as a side

1kg (2lb 4oz) baby potatoes, scrubbed

4 eggs

salt and freshly ground black pepper

For the tartare dressing

10 cornichons

1 heaped tablespoon capers

small handful of dill (15g/½oz), chopped, plus extra to garnish

small handful of flat leaf parsley (15g/½oz), finely chopped, plus extra to garnish

1 garlic clove, grated

juice of ½ lemon

3 tablespoons mayonnaise

1 teaspoon Dijon mustard

4 dashes of Worcestershire sauce

To serve

1 small onion, very finely chopped

a few anchovy fillets in oil, drained (optional)

good-quality extra virgin olive oil

1. Cook the potatoes in a large pan of salted boiling water for 10–15 minutes (depending on their size) until just tender. Transfer them from the water to a colander, leaving the water boiling in the pan, and set aside to steam.

2. Cook the eggs in the boiling potato water for 6½ minutes. Scoop them out and place in cold water to stop them cooking any further, then shell and cut into halves or quarters.

3. To make the tartare dressing, thinly slice 6 of the cornichons, then add to a large bowl (so that you can toss the potatoes in it later) with all the remaining ingredients, season with salt and pepper and mix together.

4. Now give the potatoes a good shake in the colander to rough up the edges slightly, as this will allow the dressing to cling to them. Add the potatoes to the bowl with the dressing and toss together.

5. Pile the potato salad on to a serving platter or bowl and top with the remaining 4 chopped cornichons, the extra dill and parsley, salt and freshly cracked black pepper, the chopped onion and the boiled eggs. Drape over a few salty anchovy fillets, if you like, and finally drizzle with extra virgin olive oil.

FRESH KIMCHI SALAD

I do love a traditional fermented kimchi. But if you don't have a Mason jar and the luxury of planning your meals a week in advance yet still want a pungent Korean-inspired hit, this salad is for you. I've used ssamjang as the base flavour, a thick, spicy fermented soya bean paste similar to gochujang but with more umami. I love both, but the former works best in this salad if you can get it.

....

Serves 2 as a side

½ Chinese cabbage

2 carrots

¼ daikon

4 spring onions

large pinch of salt

juice of 1 lime

2 tablespoons roasted salted peanuts, to garnish

For the ssamjang dressing

2 tablespoons soy sauce

1 heaped tablespoon ssamjang or gochujang

1 tablespoon rice vinegar

1 tablespoon fish sauce

2-cm (¾-inch) piece of fresh root ginger, peeled and grated

3 garlic cloves, finely grated

1. Shred the cabbage into thin ribbons and add to a large bowl.

2. Peel and cut the carrots and daikon into matchsticks 5mm (¼ inch) thick and add to the bowl.

3. Separate the white and green parts of the spring onions, then finely slice the greens and set aside for later. Thinly slice the whites into long strips and add to the bowl with the cabbage, carrots and daikon.

4. Add the salt and lime juice and give the veg a really good mix, scrunching them with your hands, then leave it to sit for 10 minutes to soften a little.

5. Mix the dressing ingredients together in a small bowl, then add to the veg, tossing it all together with your hands to make sure everything is well coated.

6. Crush the peanuts using a pestle and mortar until some are fine and some are still chunky.

7. Spoon the salad into a serving bowl and top with the peanuts and spring onion greens.

TWO SMACKED CUCUMBER SALADS

Stop slicing cucumbers and start smacking them! The first of my smacked cucumber recipes is inspired by a salad that Jack and I have been eating for years at China Sichuan, a local Chinese restaurant; their 'Mala' cucumber salad almost rings your tongue and lips with the numbing Sichuan peppercorns and chilli heat. I find it so addictive. I've toned down the spiciness to ensure I don't upset you, but feel free to increase the chilli powder in the Sichuan peppercorn dressing for a proper authentic hit! The second treatment is one that can be quickly assembled using jarred products, or use my homemade Crispy Chilli Oil (see page 199). Both variations of this salad will sit well, so you can make them up to an hour before serving.

....

Serves 2 as a side

1 large cucumber

salt

1. Using the side of your knife and palm of your hand, smack your cucumber from top to bottom, turning as you go to loosen the insides.
2. Slice unevenly into irregular chunks, as this is a salad that looks best messy. Add to a bowl with a big pinch of salt and leave to sit for 10 minutes.

....

For 'Mala' Sichuan

2 spring onions, green parts only, finely sliced diagonally

1 quantity Sichuan Peppercorn Dressing (see page 197)

1 tablespoon white sesame seeds

1 teaspoon chilli oil (optional)

(Pictured opposite): Add 4 tablespoons of the Sichuan peppercorn dressing to the salted cucumber and toss together so that it's all coated. (Keep the rest of the dressing in the fridge to use with the Slow-roasted Celeriac on page 65.) Spoon on to a plate, making sure you get all the dressing from the bowl, then top with the spring onion, sesame seeds, another pinch of salt and the chilli oil, if using.

....

For chilli crisp & tahini

1–2 tablespoons Crispy Chilli Oil (see page 199), or add however much you like

2 tablespoons tahini

finely grated zest and juice of ½ lime

(Pictured on page 32): Add the crispy chilli oil to the salted cucumber, making sure you get equal amounts of crispy bits and oil, and mix together so that it's all well coated. Spoon on to a plate, including all the dressing from the bowl, then drizzle over the tahini and finish with the lime zest and juice and another pinch of salt.

COURGETTE WITH PISTACHIO ZA'ATAR

We are always playing around with ideas in our test kitchen. Many of them don't make their way to our menu, frankly, as it's a complex operation to launch a single product across so many locations. Pickled courgette with za'atar was one of those ideas that got away, but stayed with me. If you want to turn this into a lovely green salad, just skip the ricotta part and toss the pickle through some crispy Little Gem lettuce with the za'atar, sliced spring onion and green chilli and a little drizzle of olive oil. If you don't have time to make the pistachio za'atar from scratch, just mix 3 tablespoons of shop-bought za'atar with 30g (1oz) of crushed roasted, salted shelled pistachios, then taste and season depending on the saltiness of the nuts.

Serves 2 as a side

1 garlic clove, finely grated
250g (9oz) ricotta cheese
extra virgin olive oil, for drizzling

For the pickled courgette strips

2 courgettes, any colour
4 tablespoons rice vinegar
1 tablespoon sugar
1 teaspoon flaky sea salt
110ml (3¾fl oz) boiling water

For the pistachio za'atar

2 tablespoons white sesame seeds
30g (1oz) shelled pistachios, crushed
2 teaspoons ground cumin
2 tablespoons sumac
2 tablespoons dried oregano
salt

1. First make the pickled courgette strips. Thinly slice the courgettes lengthways into strips using a vegetable peeler. Set aside while you make the pickle liquor.

2. Stir together the vinegar, sugar, flaky salt and boiling water in a heatproof bowl, then give it a good whisk until the sugar and salt have dissolved. Allow to cool completely. Once the pickle liquor has cooled, add the courgettes and set aside to pickle for 30 minutes.

3. To make the pistachio za'atar, toast the sesame seeds and pistachios in a dry frying pan over a medium heat for about 2 minutes until lightly golden. Add the cumin, then turn off the heat and allow it to toast in the residual heat. Transfer to a small bowl and mix together with the sumac, oregano and a pinch of salt. Set aside.

4. When ready to serve, add the grated garlic to the ricotta and give it a good stir until creamy.

5. Add a dollop of the ricotta to a serving plate, followed by the pickled courgette strips and a generous scattering of the za'atar, finishing with a drizzle of extra virgin olive oil.

SALSA VERDE PEAS, ASPARAGUS & RICOTTA

This salad is best made when asparagus is bang in season. Peas, on the other hand, are fantastic from frozen, but if you have the time to pod a batch of fresh peas, be my guest.

Serves 4 as a side

1 bunch of asparagus, about 250g (9oz)

250g (9oz) frozen peas

1 garlic clove, finely grated

finely grated zest and juice of ½ lemon

250g (9oz) ricotta cheese

small handful of mint, leaves picked

salt and freshly ground black pepper

For the salsa verde

2 anchovy fillets in oil, finely chopped

1 shallot, finely chopped

handful of flat leaf parsley (about 10g/¼oz), finely chopped

handful of basil (about 10g/¼oz), finely chopped

1 tablespoon capers, finely chopped

2 cornichons, finely chopped

1 garlic clove, grated

2 pickled guindilla peppers, finely chopped, plus 1 tablespoon brine from the jar (or alternatively, 2 tablespoons pickled chopped jalapeños)

5 tablespoons extra virgin olive oil

1 tablespoon white wine vinegar

1 tablespoon Dijon mustard

juice of ½ lemon

1. Start by making the salsa verde. Mix all the ingredients together in a bowl, seasoning with salt and black pepper, until you have a nice chunky texture.

2. Break the tough ends off the asparagus and discard, then chop the stalks into chunks.

3. Bring a pan of salted water to the boil. Add the peas and asparagus together and boil for 2 minutes (no longer!), then drain and place in a bowl of iced water to keep them bright green and fresh.

4. Stir the garlic and lemon juice into the ricotta.

5. Drain the green vegetables from the iced water, then toss in 3 tablespoons of the salsa verde.

6. Spread the ricotta on to a serving plate, and pile on the green vegetables. Tear the mint leaves and scatter over, then spoon over the remaining salsa verde and season with salt, pepper and the lemon zest to finish.

PIQUILLO PEPPERS, GOATS' CHEESE & CRUSHED PISTACHIOS

I love the little stuffed piquillo peppers you get in Spanish tapas bars. The inspiration for this salad came from a very delicious tapa I enjoyed in my favourite bar in Barcelona, El Xampanyet. You can, of course, go to the trouble of roasting your own piquillo peppers, but jarred ones are equally delicious and make this salad very quick to prepare if you're under time pressure. And, like all good Spanish dishes, this dish is best accompanied with bread.

Serves 4 as a side

150g (5½oz) soft goats' cheese

3 tablespoons extra virgin olive oil, plus extra to finish

230g (8oz) jarred piquillo peppers, the best quality you can find

handful of dill, roughly chopped

50g (1¾oz) shelled roasted salted pistachios, roughly crushed or chopped

salt and freshly ground black pepper

1. Add the goats' cheese to a small bowl with the extra virgin olive oil and give it a mix so that it loosens.

2. Drain the peppers from the jar and spread them out on a large serving platter.

3. Spoon the goats' cheese on top of the peppers, then sprinkle over the dill and the crushed pistachios.

4. Drizzle with a little extra virgin olive oil and season with salt and pepper before serving.

TOMATO & BREAD SALAD

For me, the best part of a really great tomato salad is mopping up the last few droplets of vinaigrette with some bread – the pinnacle moment that one person at the table gets to enjoy – well, this salad is basically a plate of that final bite for everyone. The key here is to source the best-quality ingredients you possibly can – the better the tomatoes, the more flavourful this salad will be. So wait until summer when tomatoes are at their sun-ripened best: heirloom, cherry, plum – use whatever looks ripe and delicious … or maybe just book a flight to Spain and go straight to the market. I like to use a good-quality sourdough that's on its second or third day and has dried out a little bit, which means it is primed to soak up all the tomato juice.

Serves 2 as a main, 4 as a side

300g (10½oz) in-season mixed tomatoes

4 tablespoons good-quality olive oil, plus extra for drizzling

1 garlic clove, finely chopped

large handful of basil leaves

1 tablespoon red wine vinegar

1 tablespoon runny honey

½ red onion, finely sliced into half-moons

juice of 1 lemon

200g (7oz) sourdough bread, torn into chunks

10 good-quality anchovy fillets in oil

salt

1. Slice or chop the tomatoes into bite-sized pieces and add to a large bowl with a big pinch of salt, 2 tablespoons of the olive oil, the chopped garlic, basil leaves, vinegar and honey. Toss together, then set aside for 10 minutes.

2. Place the red onion in a separate bowl, squeeze over the lemon juice and add a pinch of salt. Using your hands, scrunch the onion to ensure it's fully coated, then set aside to pickle for a few minutes. The onion should turn lightly pink but still retain a little bite.

3. Add the sourdough and the remaining olive oil to the bowl with the tomatoes, and using your hands gently toss to ensure the bread soaks up the dressing.

4. Tip the salad on to a serving dish, top with the pickled onion and any juices, then drape over the anchovy fillets. Finish with an extra drizzle of olive oil, if required.

A CHERRY SALAD

I've always been more of a savoury person than sweet. So, when it comes to making a fruit salad, I think it's fun to add salty, spicy and sour notes to bounce off the natural sweetness. This recipe was inspired by a simple cherry salad I ate at the restaurant HaBasta in Tel Aviv. I sat at the bar alone with a very large smile on my face, watching the pass as the kitchen sent out exciting dishes using seasonal ingredients from the nearby vegetable market. I had some of my most memorable dishes that night, and this dish is a reminder of the emotional impact food can have and why I love it so much.

Serves 4–6 as a side

200g (7oz) cherries

200g (7oz) piccolo tomatoes, halved

200g (7oz) red grapes, halved

2–3 fresh jalapeños or other green chillies, sliced

1–2 garlic cloves, grated (to taste)

2 tablespoons red wine vinegar

5 tablespoons extra virgin olive oil

large handful of fresh coriander, leaves picked

large pinch of flaky sea salt

1. Start by pitting your cherries with either a cherry pitter if you have one, or by cutting around the stone, twisting to separate in half and removing the stone with your fingers.

2. Place the cherries in a large mixing bowl and add the tomatoes, grapes, jalapeños, garlic, vinegar and a big pinch of salt. Give it a mix and leave to sit for 10 minutes.

3. Once the fruits have released some of their natural juices, stir in the extra virgin olive oil. You should have a nice pink liquid forming at the bottom of the bowl.

4. At the last minute, toss through the coriander leaves and taste for seasoning, adding more salt if needed. Serve on a large rimmed serving plate and enjoy.

WATERMELON, FETA & SPICED PUMPKIN SEEDS

Make this if you can get your hands on a ripe watermelon – this sweet, salty, spicy and savoury salad is a great way to use it on a piping hot day!

Serves 2 as a main, 4 as a side

1 small very ripe watermelon

1 red onion

small handful of mint, leaves picked

small handful of basil, leaves picked

2 tablespoons extra virgin olive oil

juice of 1 lime

100g (3½oz) feta cheese

1 quantity Maple Spiced Pumpkin Seeds (see page 196)

pinch of chilli flakes

salt

1. Peel the watermelon, slice into small wedges and place them in a large mixing bowl.

2. Very finely slice the red onion and add to the bowl with the watermelon.

3. Add the herbs to the bowl, then season with salt. Drizzle over the extra virgin olive oil and lime juice, then toss to coat everything.

4. Tip on to a large plate or platter and break the feta into pieces over the salad.

5. Scatter with a generous handful of the maple spiced pumpkin seeds and the chilli flakes, then serve.

SOUR GRAPES, FLAKED ALMONDS & RICOTTA

Grapes are an underused fruit when it comes to salads. They are of course delicious just halved in a simple salad, but try giving them the charring or roasting treatment for a gooey and juicy result. For another alternative to add to your repertoire, we are pickling them in this recipe! As well as rendering the fruit lovely and sweet, the pickling process gives them a pleasing sourness, perfectly complemented by the sweet toasted almonds and creamy ricotta. Serve the grapes warm as a nice contrast to the cold ricotta; adding some of the pink pickling liquid to their dressing gives them an extra edge of acidity.

....

Serves 4 as a starter or a side

handful of flaked almonds

½ garlic clove, finely grated

250g (9oz) ricotta cheese

2 tablespoons extra virgin olive oil

For the pickled grapes

240ml (8½fl oz) white wine vinegar

240ml (8½fl oz) water

4 tablespoons sugar

1 teaspoon salt

500g (1lb 2oz) seedless red or white grapes, or any type you like

1. To make the pickled grapes, heat the vinegar, water, sugar and salt in a saucepan over a medium heat and simmer for a few minutes. Add the grapes and simmer for another 2 minutes, then turn off the heat and set aside for about 15 minutes to cool in the liquid.

2. Meanwhile, toast the flaked almonds in a small dry frying pan over a medium heat for 1–2 minutes until lightly golden, then remove from the heat and set aside to cool.

3. Stir the grated garlic into the ricotta.

4. Reheat the grapes and then scoop them out of the pickle liquor and dress with the extra virgin olive oil and 1 tablespoon of the pickle liquor.

5. Dollop the ricotta on to a serving plate or platter, and top with the pickled grapes and toasted almonds.

'SWEET & SOUR' PLUM & TOMATO

Kiln is one of my favourite places to eat when I'm in Central London's Soho – a high-energy Thai restaurant with an open kitchen. Woks frying over embers, grilling and smoking, create deep-tasting Thai curries and broths; it's the kind of place that gets my heart pumping. Typically (as I often get excited by the simplest of things), it was a plum in fish fragrance salad that stood out for me the last time I was there, and this recipe is inspired by that memorable experience. Make this in summer when the tomatoes and plums are at their peak sweetness – it'll make all the difference. The fish sauce dressing is one of the most intensely umami and addictive sauces ever, so I always have a batch of it in my fridge – it will keep for a month after you make it. It's pungent and spicy, but balanced by the naturally sweet tomato and plum. Yum.

Serves 4 as a side

2 large good-quality heirloom tomatoes

4 ripe plums

small handful of mint leaves

flaky sea salt

For the fish sauce dressing

2 tablespoons fish sauce

juice of 1 lime

½ tablespoon maple syrup or palm sugar

1 garlic clove, finely grated

1 green bird's-eye chilli, very finely sliced

1 red bird's-eye chilli, very finely sliced

1. Bring a large pan of water to the boil. Cut a small cross in the top of each tomato and add to the boiling water for 30 seconds–1 minute, then drain and place in a bowl of iced water.

2. Cut the plums in half and remove the stones, then chop them into bite-sized pieces and add to a bowl.

3. Peel off the skins of the tomatoes, which should all come off easily. Cut the tomatoes into similar-sized pieces to the plums. Sprinkle over a pinch of flaky sea salt, then add to the bowl with the plums.

4. Add all the dressing ingredients to the bowl with the tomatoes and plums and give everything a good toss so that the fruit is all well coated. (You may want to adjust the seasoning depending on when you're eating this – the better the tomatoes and plums, the less sugar you'll need.)

5. Let them sit for 10 minutes so that all their natural juices are drawn out. Add the mint leaves and then give the bowl another stir, before pouring the tomatoes and plums on to a plate to serve.

BLOOD ORANGE & BURRATA (OR PAUL'S SALAD)

My mum has a holiday house in Castletown, County Wexford with a perfect view of the sea, which has been in our family since I was born. As it's not within walking distance of any pubs or restaurants, we tend to bring as much food in the car with us, then I'm tasked with feeding everybody. On one occasion, just before I started developing the recipes for this book, my stepdad Paul offered to make the starter. A fruit salad recipe was on his mind, but halfway through preparing it a gin and tonic was also on his mind, so I was called upon to finish the job for him. This being a house with very little in the larder, it forced me to keep it simple. I had lemons, good olive oil, a nephew whom I instructed to twist black pepper until his arms were sore and some wilting Thai basil, plus a pot of stracciatella cheese (the creamy filling in burrata). Not so bad now that I write it. It blew my mum away and Paul was chuffed to have been a part of it. A lovely light starter coming into spring.

....

Serves 4 as a side or as a starter

3 oranges (I used a mix of regular and blood oranges, but you can use any kind)

1 ripe mango

1 red onion

200g (7oz) ball of burrata cheese

small handful of Thai basil or regular basil leaves

For the black pepper vinaigrette

2 tablespoons extra virgin olive oil

juice of ½ lemon

1 tablespoon red wine vinegar

1½ teaspoons runny honey

pinch of flaky sea salt

lots of freshly ground black pepper

1. Slice off the top and bottom of the oranges, then peel the skin off with a sharp serrated knife, removing as much of the white pith as you can. Slice the oranges into rounds 1cm (½ inch) thick.

2. Slice off the skin of the mango, then cut the flesh into evenly sized pieces, discarding the stone.

3. Thinly slice the red onion into rounds and arrange on a serving platter together with the orange slices and mango pieces.

4. To make the dressing, add all the ingredients to a small bowl, finishing with A LOT of black pepper – I like to add about 20 twists. Whisk together, then taste and adjust the seasoning.

5. Break the burrata on to the platter, then add the basil followed by the dressing.

VEGETABLES ARE CENTRE OF ATTENTION

SLOW-ROASTED CELERIAC WITH SICHUAN PEPPERCORN DRESSING & SPRING ONION SALSA

I made an Ottolenghi recipe for a bunch of friends at cookery school a few years ago that called for slow-roasting a whole celeriac, which I misread and just roasted celeriac wedges in the oven on a high heat. My friends and I were delighted. So if you don't have time to slow-roast, don't fear, but for seriously special results do it! The flavour develops over time in the same way as a slow-roasted shoulder of pork, with the natural sugars slowly seeping out and creating a caramel-like syrup that you continually baste the celeriac with throughout cooking. Such a humble vegetable can really impress when prepared in the right way. You can easily double this recipe, or take the opportunity to slow-roast a few whole garlic bulbs while the oven is on.

Serves 4 as a side

1 celeriac, about 1kg (2lb 4oz)

100ml (3½fl oz) olive oil

½ teaspoon fine salt

1 quantity Sichuan Peppercorn Dressing (see page 197)

flaky sea salt, to finish

For the spring onion salsa

4 spring onions, thinly sliced

small handful of fresh coriander (15g/½oz)

1 green chilli, deseeded and finely sliced

finely grated zest and juice of 1 lime, plus extra zest to serve

1. Preheat the oven to 190°C (170°C fan, 375°F), Gas Mark 5.

2. Trim off any hairy roots from the celeriac, then wash and dry thoroughly. Pierce all over with a fork (about 30 or so times) so that it cooks evenly.

3. Pour the olive oil into a low-sided roasting tray. Roll the celeriac in the oil until it's evenly coated, then season all over with the fine salt. Roast for 2 hours, basting with the oil and syrupy celeriac juices every 30 minutes until it's a deeply roasted nutty brown and has shrunk in size.

4. Remove the celeriac from the oven and turn the oven up to 240°C (220°C fan, 475°F), Gas Mark 9.

5. Carefully cut the celeriac into 8 wedges by cutting in half through the middle, then into quarters and again into eighths.

6. Sit the celeriac wedges back in the roasting tray and paint each side with the remaining juices from the pan. Season with salt and roast for another 20 minutes, turning over halfway through once the exposed sides have coloured.

7. Meanwhile, toss all the salsa ingredients together in a bowl and set aside.

8. Transfer the celeriac wedges to a serving plate and spoon over half the Sichuan peppercorn dressing, followed by the salsa. Finally grate over the extra lime zest and add a little flaky sea salt to finish.

OLIVE OIL-BRAISED FENNEL WITH CHORIZO & HALLOUMI HONEY

Chorizo, halloumi, grapes and honey! This combination could be taken in many ways: tossed together with rocket and lemon and you've got a fab salad, or serve with fish and you've got a great main dish. Here, the braised fennel is tender and elegant – the perfect bed for the spicy, sweet and salty topping.

Serves 4

2 fennel bulbs

1 lemon

100ml (3½fl oz) extra virgin olive oil

pinch of salt

1 tablespoon fennel seeds

100g (3½oz) chorizo sausage

225g (8oz) block of halloumi cheese

1 tablespoon olive oil

250g (9oz) red grapes

freshly ground black pepper

small handful of basil leaves, to garnish

For the honey & garlic dressing

1 garlic clove, finely grated

2 tablespoons runny honey

2 tablespoons red wine vinegar

1. Trim off the stalks of the fennel bulbs, keeping any fronds to garnish, then the root ends. Slice the fennel into wedges 2cm (¾ inch) thick (each one into roughly 8 wedges).

2. Slice the lemon into rounds 5mm (¼ inch) thick, then put in a large, deep pot with a lid along with the fennel wedges. Add the extra virgin olive oil and salt, then pour over just enough water to cover everything. Place over a high heat and bring to the boil, then once boiling, turn the heat down to a simmer and cook for 15–20 minutes until the fennel is soft and tender. Drain, add back to the pot and cover with the lid to keep warm.

3. While the fennel is cooking, toast the fennel seeds in a medium nonstick frying pan over a medium-high heat for 1 minute. Remove the pan from the heat and transfer the fennel seeds to a mortar to cool. Once cooled, lightly crush with a pestle.

4. Remove the skin from the chorizo, then cut into 1-cm (½-inch) thick slices. Cut the halloumi into similar-sized pieces and set aside.

5. Once the frying pan has cooled down, add the chorizo along with the olive oil, place over a medium heat and fry for 4 minutes until crisp on both sides and its oil has been released. Now add the halloumi and grapes to the pan and allow to cook in the juices for a few minutes until golden. Turn off the heat and add the crushed fennel seeds along with all the dressing ingredients, then toss so that everything is well coated.

6. Add the cooked fennel to a serving platter, then spoon over the dressed chorizo mixture. Finish with the basil, fennel fronds if you have any and freshly ground black pepper.

TANGY TOMS & ROASTED AUBERGINE

One of my favourite side dishes, the gooey aubergine with the crispy garlic is a textural delight and the kind of food I get really excited about. The tomato sauce is tangy, sour and spicy, and comes together in no time. There are many other directions in which you could take this sauce – try adding a protein like prawns for a quick dinner with rice or noodles.

Serves 4 as a side

2 aubergines

6 tablespoons olive oil

6 garlic cloves, very finely sliced

salt

For the tangy tomato sauce

250g (9oz) cherry tomatoes

4-cm (1½-inch) piece of fresh root ginger, peeled

1 habanero or Scotch bonnet chilli

200ml (7fl oz) water

generous pinch of salt

1 teaspoon sugar

1 teaspoon rice vinegar

1 tablespoon fish sauce, or soy sauce to make it vegan

To serve

small handful of chives, finely chopped

1 lime, cut into wedges

flaky sea salt

1. Preheat the oven to 240°C (220°C fan, 475°F), Gas Mark 9.

2. Slice the aubergines into rounds 2cm (¾ inch) thick. Lay them in a low-sided roasting tray, drizzle with 2 tablespoons of the olive oil and season generously with salt. Roast for 25 minutes, turning halfway through, until they are golden brown and soft in the middle.

3. Meanwhile, set a sieve over a heatproof bowl. Add the remaining 4 tablespoons of olive oil to a frying pan, then add the garlic with a pinch of salt to the cold oil. Place over a medium-low heat and heat the oil up gently with the garlic in it (this is the key to avoid burning the garlic). Fry for 2–3 minutes until the garlic is very lightly golden. Keep an eye on it here, as once it starts to turn golden, it will quickly burn. Pour the oil and garlic into the sieve so that the bowl underneath catches the garlic oil.

4. To make the sauce, blitz the tomatoes, ginger and chilli together in a blender until smooth.

5. Add 3 tablespoons of the garlic oil back to the frying pan along with the blitzed tomato mixture, place over a high heat and allow to bubble rapidly for 30 seconds. Pour in the measured water, add the salt and sugar and bring to a simmer, then turn down the heat a little and allow to bubble away for about 15 minutes until the sauce is reduced, glossy and thickened. Now stir in the vinegar and fish sauce or soy sauce.

6. To serve, add the tomato sauce to a serving plate and top with the roasted aubergines and crispy garlic. Finish with the chopped chives, a squeeze of lime juice from the wedges, an extra drizzle of the leftover garlic oil and a little flaky sea salt.

CHARRED BROCCOLI WITH ROMESCO & SPICY ALMONDS

Romesco is a sauce, a dip and a friend, and something that I make regularly. It goes great with the broccoli in addition to the traditional pairing with charred baby leeks of Catalonia. Make extra and use as a spread on toast, or serve with a piece of salmon or as a pasta sauce. It's rich and nutty, but the sherry vinegar brings a tart acidity that I love.

Serves 4 as a side

50g (1¾oz) flaked almonds

2 tablespoons olive oil

250g (9oz) Tenderstem broccoli

juice of ½ lemon

charred sourdough bread, to serve

For the paprika salt

1 teaspoon sweet paprika

¾ teaspoon fine salt

½ teaspoon cayenne pepper

½ teaspoon caster sugar

For the romesco

50g (1¾oz) blanched hazelnuts

50g (1¾oz) blanched almonds

6 red peppers

1 garlic bulb

1 teaspoon smoked paprika

3 tablespoons extra virgin olive oil, plus extra to finish

½ tablespoon sherry vinegar, or to taste

salt and freshly ground black pepper

1. Preheat the oven to 200°C (180°C fan, 400°F), Gas Mark 6. Mix the paprika salt ingredients together in a small bowl. Add the flaked almonds with 1 tablespoon of the olive oil and mix until well coated. Spread the almond mixture out on a baking tray and roast for 5 minutes until lightly golden. Tip on to a cold tray to stop them cooking any further and set aside to cool. Leave the oven on.

2. For the romesco, spread out the blanched hazelnuts and almonds on the baking tray you used for the almond flakes and roast for 8 minutes until golden. Remove from the oven and set aside to cool.

3. Increase the oven temperature to 220°C (200°C fan, 425°F), Gas Mark 7.

4. Place the peppers on a baking tray, then wrap the garlic bulb in foil and add it to the tray. Roast the peppers for 25 minutes until their skins are charred and loose. Remove the tray from the oven, then transfer the peppers to a bowl, place a plate over the top to cover completely and set aside to steam for 10 minutes.

5. When your peppers have finished steaming, peel off the charred skins, which should all come off easily. Pull off the stalks and remove the seeds, then add the peppers to a blender. Squeeze out the roasted garlic flesh from their skins into the blender, then add the roasted hazelnuts, almonds and the remaining romesco ingredients and blitz.

6. For the broccoli, trim off the woody ends and drizzle with the remaining 1 tablespoon of olive oil. Heat a griddle pan over a high heat. Once hot, lay the broccoli in the pan and char for 4 minutes on each side until it's a little blackened in places (the timing may differ depending on the type of broccoli). Remove from the heat, squeeze over the lemon juice and season with a big pinch of salt.

7. Spread the romesco on to a serving plate or platter, then lay the charred broccoli on top. Sprinkle with the paprika salted almond flakes and drizzle with a little extra virgin olive oil. Serve with a stack of charred sourdough to mop up the remaining sauce. Any leftover paprika salted almonds can be stored in an airtight container where they will keep for up to 1 week.

COURGETTES, WHIPPED FETA & CRISPY CHILLI OIL

The technique of charring the courgettes and then roasting them here really brings out their natural savoury flavour, making the very best of this everyday vegetable. Whipped feta is one of the most moreish umami things you can eat, and anything topped with crispy garlic and chilli is sure to pique my interest! You'll have some of the garlic and chilli oil left over, and if you keep reading this book, you won't need me to tell you what to do with it. But just to mention that it's great for salad dressings, drizzling over pizza, tossing with pasta or frying an egg.

....

Serves 2–4 as a side

2 courgettes

2–3 tablespoons olive oil

1 lemon, halved

small handful of oregano, leaves picked, to garnish

salt

For the crispy garlic & chilli

100ml (3½fl oz) olive oil

6 garlic cloves, finely sliced

1 red chilli, finely sliced into rounds

For the whipped feta

150g (5½oz) feta cheese

2 tablespoons cold water

2 tablespoons extra virgin olive oil

1. Preheat the oven to 200°C (180°C fan, 400°F), Gas Mark 6.

2. Cut the courgettes in half lengthways and score the cut sides in a crisscross pattern. Pour over the olive oil, season with salt and rub it in with your hands so that all the surfaces are well coated.

3. Heat a large frying pan over a high heat. Once hot, add the courgettes, cut-sides down, and fry for 3–4 minutes until the flesh is charred and blackened (you may need to do this in batches, depending on the size of your pan) – you aren't cooking them all the way through here, just getting some colour and flavour before roasting them. Transfer the courgettes to a large, low-sided roasting tray and roast for 10–15 minutes until tender.

4. Add the lemon halves, cut-sides down, to the hot pan and char for a minute, then transfer to a plate to cool.

5. While the courgettes are roasting, prepare the crispy garlic and chilli and oil. Set a sieve over a heatproof bowl. Add the oil to a frying pan, then add the garlic and chilli with a pinch of salt to the cold oil. Place over a medium-low heat and heat the oil up gently with the garlic and chilli in it (this is the key to avoid burning the garlic). Fry for 3–4 minutes, stirring often so that the garlic slices don't stick together and cook evenly, until lightly golden. Keep an eye on it here, as once it starts to turn golden, it will quickly burn. Pour the oil, garlic and chilli into the sieve so that the bowl underneath catches the flavoured oil. We'll use this oil, so don't throw it away!

6. Blitz the feta, cold water and extra virgin olive oil in a blender until smooth and creamy, then spoon on to a serving platter. Pile on the courgettes, followed by the crispy garlic and chilli, the oregano and a drizzle of the garlic and chilli oil, then squeeze over the juice of the charred lemon.

AUBERGINES & YOGURT WITH GINGER SPRING ONION DRESSING

The same cooking technique used for the courgettes on the previous page is applied here to aubergines – a quick char for colour, followed by roasting to make them go all gooey and rich inside. It's a great way to char a vegetable without smoking out your kitchen. Spring onions and ginger are a combination I've always loved from years of eating in Chinese restaurants growing up with my dad, so I had to create a recipe with them for this book. The hot fragrant oil splitting the yogurt is the stuff of my dreams!

Serves 4 as a side

2 aubergines

75ml (2½fl oz) olive oil, plus extra for the aubergines

2 lemons, halved

1 bunch of spring onions (about 5)

5-cm (2-inch) piece of fresh root ginger

150g (5½oz) natural yogurt

salt

1. Preheat the oven to 200°C (180°C fan, 400°F), Gas Mark 6.

2. Cut the aubergines in half lengthways and score the cut sides in a crisscross pattern. Pour over 2–3 tablespoons of olive oil and rub it in with your hands so that all the surfaces are well coated.

3. Heat a large frying pan over a high heat. Once hot, add the aubergines, cut-sides down, and cook for 3–4 minutes until the flesh is charred and golden all over (you may need to do this in batches) – you aren't cooking them all the way through here, just getting some colour and flavour before roasting them. Transfer the aubergines to a large, low-sided roasting tray, drizzle with a little more olive oil and roast for 15–20 minutes until soft.

4. Add the lemon halves, cut-sides down, to the hot pan to char for a minute, then transfer to a plate to cool.

5. Finely slice the spring onions into long strips, then peel and slice the ginger into long, thin matchsticks roughly the same size as the spring onions so that they cook in a similar time. (It'll look like a lot, but it all cooks down and you'll be sad you didn't do more, so double the recipe if you're smart!)

6. Set a metal sieve over a heatproof bowl. Put 75ml (2½ fl oz) olive oil in a saucepan with the spring onions, ginger and a pinch of salt and place over a medium heat. Once the oil starts to bubble, stir it and allow the spring onions and ginger to gently fry for 8–10 minutes until evenly golden and the ginger has started to curl up, looks a little frazzly and is crispy. Pour the oil, spring onions and ginger into the sieve so that the bowl underneath catches the flavoured oil.

7. Mix 3 tablespoons of the flavoured oil (reserve the rest for stir-fries, dressings or frying an egg) with the juice of one charred lemon in a bowl and season with salt. Add the crispy spring onions and ginger to the dressing and toss to coat.

8. Spoon the yogurt on to a large serving platter, then lay the aubergines on top, followed by the crispy spring onions and ginger with all the dressing. Finally, squeeze over the juice of the remaining charred lemon to finish.

BRAISED COURGETTE CACIO E PEPE

Cacio e pepe is probably my favourite pasta dish of all time. Heavy on the black pepper and pecorino, it's so beautifully simple. I've drawn on that classic Italian concept to create this special vegetable recipe. I'm not about to tell you that courgetti pasta is better than spaghetti, because it's not! But something magical happens when you braise courgettes in their own juices. This could be thrown through pasta, as the courgettes become quite jammy and soft, but it's stunning as a side dish. The recipe can easily be doubled or tripled depending on the size of your cooking pot.

....

Serves 2 as a side

2 courgettes

3 tablespoons good-quality olive oil

small handful of basil leaves (about 15g/½oz)

2 garlic cloves, peeled and smashed with the side of a knife

generous pinch of salt

20g (¾oz) pecorino cheese, plus extra to serve

lots of freshly ground black pepper

squeeze of lemon juice, to serve

1. Cut the courgettes into discs about 5mm (¼ inch) thick. Place a heavy-based flameproof casserole or saucepan with a lid over the lowest heat you can. Add the olive oil and the courgettes, the basil and the whole garlic cloves along with the salt. Stir it all together, then cover the pan with the lid and cook very, very gently for 30 minutes. The courgettes shouldn't fry or be getting any colour, but mostly steaming in the moisture coming from them. Lift the lid to check on them from time to time, gently stirring them around to make sure they all cook evenly.

2. Discard the wilted basil leaves and garlic (or remove and mash the garlic into a paste, then add it back to the pan), then grate in the pecorino, add 20 grinds of black pepper and very gently stir into the courgettes.

3. Spoon the braised courgettes on to a serving plate and serve with an extra grating of pecorino, a little extra black pepper and a squeeze of lemon juice.

BUTTERNUT SQUASH WITH WALNUT PESTO & FETA

I get most of my recipe ideas from past experiences or memories, and this one came from a butternut squash bruschetta with these flavours that I enjoyed years ago and it stuck with me. The sweetness of the squash contrasts nicely with the tangy, spicy pesto and salty feta. It's lovely for a warm winter salad, but could be baked into a pasta dish or bulked out with cannellini beans.

Serves 2–4 as a side

1 butternut squash, about 1kg (2lb 4oz)

3 tablespoons olive oil

100g (3½oz) feta cheese, sliced

salt and freshly ground black pepper

chilli flakes, to serve

For the walnut pesto

75g (2¾oz) walnuts

½ tablespoon fennel seeds

1 garlic clove, peeled

15g (½oz) Parmesan cheese, freshly grated

large handful of basil (about 20g/¾oz), plus extra leaves to serve

400g (14oz) sun-dried tomatoes, finely chopped

2 tablespoons red wine vinegar

150ml (10 tablespoons) extra virgin olive oil

1. Preheat the oven to 210°C (190°C fan, 410°F), Gas Mark 6½.

2. Cut the butternut squash in half lengthways and scoop out the seeds, then cut into chunky wedges. Place them on a baking tray, add the olive oil and a generous pinch of salt and toss with your hands until well coated. Roast for 30 minutes, turning halfway through, until golden, soft and the skin has crisped up slightly.

3. For the pesto, spread the walnuts and fennel seeds out on a separate baking tray, add to the oven with the squash and roast for 5 minutes. Remove from the oven and set aside to cool.

4. Blend the toasted walnuts and fennel seeds with the garlic, Parmesan and basil in a food processor until it becomes the texture of breadcrumbs, then add the sun-dried tomatoes, wine vinegar and half (5 tablespoons) of the extra virgin olive oil and blend again until it forms a pesto retaining some consistency.

5. Arrange the roasted squash and feta on a serving plate or platter, followed by a few generous dollops of the pesto, some extra basil and a sprinkle of chilli flakes to finish.

6. Store any remaining pesto in an airtight jar covered with the remaining 5 tablespoons of extra virgin olive oil to preserve it. It will last up to a week in the fridge.

CHARRED CABBAGE WITH LEMON TAHINI SAUCE & SUN-DRIED TOMATO SALSA

A quick side to put on a table that has tons going on. I love how well cabbage chars – you get the blackened flavour on the outside, while the layers of cabbage leaves within steam and soften a little but still retain some bite; they become rich, savoury and really attention-grabbing. The tangy, tart tomato salsa and rich tahini sauce make the humble cabbage feel quite luxurious.

Serves 4 as a side

2 sweetheart cabbages

2 tablespoons olive oil

For the lemon tahini sauce

4 tablespoons tahini

juice of ½ lemon

6 tablespoons cold water

salt and freshly ground black pepper

For the sun-dried tomato salsa

6 sun-dried tomatoes, finely chopped

1 tablespoon capers, finely chopped

1 garlic clove, very finely chopped

1 tablespoon finely chopped flat leaf parsley

juice of ½ lemon

1 tablespoon extra virgin olive oil, plus extra to serve

1 tablespoon red wine vinegar

pinch of flaky sea salt

a few grinds of black pepper

1. Start by making the lemon tahini sauce. Mix all the ingredients together in a small bowl, adding salt and pepper to taste, until you have a smooth creamy consistency.

2. Mix all the salsa ingredients together in a separate small bowl.

3. Heat a griddle pan over a high heat. Cut the cabbages into quarters to make 4 wedges, then drizzle them with the olive oil. Once hot, place the cabbage wedges in the pan, one cut-side down, and char for about 3 minutes on each cut side, or until blackened on the outside and softened inside.

4. Pour the lemon tahini sauce on to a large serving plate and place the charred cabbage on top, then spoon over the salsa in little dollops across the dish. Finish the dish with a splash of extra virgin olive oil.

STIR-FRIED SAVOY CABBAGE WITH FRIED PEANUTS & CRISPY LIME LEAVES

I love this dish, as it feels like you're eating a big bowl of cabbage-y noodles. It involves a bit of prep, but once that's done it's quick to pull together. If you don't want to matchstick the aromatics, just make sure they are in chunks and of equal size so that they don't burn. You'll have more of the fried peanuts than you need, but you'll thank me later, as they keep for a few weeks in an airtight container. Once comfortable with this dish, try adding spices and playing around with the formula depending on what you have to hand. This works great as a as a side with a Malaysian-style curry and coconut rice or as a main with a crispy fried egg.

....

Serves 4 as a side

7 garlic cloves

2 thumb-sized pieces of fresh root ginger

1 green chilli

1 bunch of spring onions (about 5)

1 Savoy cabbage

1 tablespoon soy sauce

salt

To serve

1 quantity Fried Peanuts & Crispy Lime Leaves (see page 196), oil reserved

juice of 1 lime

1. This is a stir-fried dish, so it's best to have everything prepped before turning on the wok.

2. Peel and finely slice the garlic. Peel the ginger, then cut into thin matchsticks along with the green chilli and spring onions. Set aside separately on a plate.

3. Cut the cabbage in half, then into quarters to make 4 thick wedges. Remove the core, then shred all the cabbage into thin strips and set aside.

4. Pour the reserved peanut and lime leaf cooking oil into the wok and heat over a high heat. Add the garlic, ginger, green chilli and a pinch of salt to the hot oil so that it all sizzles together. Fry for about 2–3 minutes, stirring as you cook, then stir in the spring onions for a further minute.

5. Now begin adding the cabbage in stages, as you don't want to overcrowd the wok. Toss the first batch to coat in the flavoured oil and aromatics, leave to cook untouched for 20 seconds so that the edges get crispy and then toss again before adding another handful of cabbage. Repeat this process until all the cabbage is in the wok. You want to end up with some charred crispy bits as well as some fresh crunchy green strands.

6. Once the last bit of cabbage is in, toss it together and then let it sit in the pan for another few minutes off the heat until it has all softened and you don't have any raw bits, and it's all still vibrantly green.

7. Add the soy sauce and give it a final toss. Pile into a serving bowl, then add the fried peanuts and crispy lime leaves on top. Serve with a big squeeze of lime juice.

CHAAT POTATOES WITH TAMARIND YOGURT & PICKLES

This recipe is a play on the much-popularized fried chaat potatoes found at Indian street markets. While the closest I've got to India was a flight transfer in Mumbai, one of my favourite local Indian grocery stores Kwality Foods (and that does mean 'quality'!) supplies an array of beautiful spice blends that I love, including the addictive tangy, sour and salty chaat masala. A side dish we have been serving in the restaurants for a few years now, this combination of crispy chaat potatoes, tart tamarind yogurt and sweet and spicy pickled chillies is spectacular. I recommend making this as part of an Indian-themed dinner – a potato dish that will grab the attention of the room.

Serves 4 as a side

1kg (2lb 4oz) baby potatoes, scrubbed

2 tablespoons chaat masala

4 tablespoons sunflower oil

handful of fresh coriander, roughly chopped, to serve

½ quantity Pickled Shallots & Chillies (see page 201)

salt

For the tamarind yogurt

6 tablespoons natural yogurt

1 tablespoon tamarind paste

1 tablespoon mayonnaise

1 teaspoon runny honey

1 teaspoon ground cumin

2-cm (¾-inch) piece of fresh root ginger, peeled and grated

1 garlic clove, finely grated

pinch of flaky sea salt, or more to taste

1. Preheat the oven to 220°C (200°C fan, 425°F), Gas Mark 7.

2. Cut the baby potatoes in half lengthways so that you have nice long wedges. Add to a large bowl along with the chaat masala, sunflower oil and about ⅓ teaspoon of salt, then mix together so that the potatoes are completely coated.

3. Spread the potatoes out, cut-sides down, on a large baking tray (so that they are taking direct heat from the pan, which ensures maximum crispiness), then bake for 20–30 minutes, untouched, until they have a crispy exterior and a soft, fluffy interior.

4. Mix all the tamarind yogurt ingredients together in a bowl and taste for seasoning – depending on the brand of tamarind you're using, it might need more salt. It should be tart and creamy, but with the little touch of honey bringing balance.

5. Pour the tamarind yogurt on to a large serving plate and spread out. Scatter with the chopped fresh coriander, then arrange the crispy potatoes on top. Sprinkle the pickled shallots and chillies and a little spoonful of the pickle liquor across the dish– this last step really brings the dish to life.

BLISTERED GARLICKY GREEN BEANS

There's some deep-frying happening here, but it's just to blister the green beans a little. For the sauce, I strongly recommend you get hold of Golden Mountain Seasoning Sauce, as it's great to have in the larder and inexpensive to buy from Thai or Asian food stores or online suppliers. If you don't have it, just add more oyster sauce, which you can find anywhere these days. I made this dish at a dinner party and received major praise. It may have been the frying, or the sauce, but it had nothing to do with wine.

Serves 4 as a side

100ml (3½fl oz) sunflower oil

400g (14oz) fine green beans, tailed

4 garlic cloves, roughly chopped

½ teaspoon sugar

For the stir-fry sauce

3 tablespoons oyster sauce

3 tablespoons Golden Mountain Seasoning Sauce (if you can get it, or use extra oyster sauce)

1 teaspoon sugar

1. Heat the sunflower oil in a wok over a high heat. Once hot, add a small batch of the beans and fry in the oil for about 30 seconds until blistered, shaking the wok to ensure they blister evenly – we are just looking to blister the skin, so don't worry about cooking them all the way through. Remove with kitchen tongs and drain on kitchen paper, then repeat the process until you have blistered all the beans.

2. To make the stir-fry sauce, add the oyster sauce and seasoning sauce (or extra oyster sauce) to a small bowl, then stir in the sugar.

3. Reserve most of the bean cooking oil in the wok, about 2 tablespoons, and reheat over a high heat. Once the oil is shimmering, add each of the following in turn and in this order: the garlic, green beans, sugar and finally the sauce. Toss to coat all the beans in the sauce and cook for 1–2 minutes until the garlic has softened and the beans have absorbed the sauce.

4. Remove from the heat and pour on to a platter to serve.

RATATOUILLE CON TOMATE

This recipe is a cross between a *ratatouille* and *pan con tomate* – the latter being one of my favourite Spanish snacks! It was born out of my apartment being too hot (yes, Ireland does get hot) and not wanting to turn my oven on, so I resorted to quickly charring aubergine and courgette in a frying pan on the hob. The dressing is simply made using grated tomatoes – so make sure you buy the best summer has to offer.

....

Serves 4 as a side

1 aubergine

1 courgette

2 tablespoons olive oil

3 large ripe tomatoes

salt and freshly ground black pepper

toasted sourdough bread, to serve

For the crispy garlic oil with oregano

4 tablespoons extra virgin olive oil

6 garlic cloves, very thinly sliced

1 heaped tablespoon oregano leaves

1. Cut the aubergine and courgette into quarters lengthways and then into batons. Add to a bowl, sprinkle over ½ tablespoon salt and toss to coat, then set aside for 10 minutes. This will draw out some of the water content, flavour the vegetables and result in a more tender, soft texture.

2. For the crispy garlic oil, set a sieve over a heatproof bowl. Add the extra virgin olive oil to a frying pan, then add the garlic with a pinch of salt to the cold oil. Place over a medium-low heat and heat the oil up gently with the garlic in it (this is the key to avoid burning the garlic). Fry for 2 minutes until very lightly golden, then add the oregano and fry for 30 seconds. Keep an eye on it here, as once the garlic starts to turn golden, it will quickly burn. Pour the oil, garlic and oregano into the sieve so that the bowl underneath catches the garlic oil.

3. Tip the aubergine and courgette on to a clean tea towel or kitchen paper and dry each side well. Place the frying pan back over a high heat. Once hot, add the aubergine and courgette to the pan and dry-fry for 4 minutes on each side until deeply charred on all sides and softened (you may need to do this in batches, depending on the size of your pan). Reduce the heat and allow the pan to cool a little, then add all the aubergines and courgettes back to the pan with the olive oil and stir for 1 minute until tender and glazed. Season with a little more salt to taste.

4. While the veg are charring, grate the tomatoes on the large side of a box grater into a bowl. Add a large pinch of salt and 2 tablespoons of the now-cooled garlic oil.

5. To assemble, spoon the grated tomatoes on a large serving platter, then place the charred aubergine and courgette on top, followed by the crispy garlic and oregano, a little more of the garlic oil and freshly ground black pepper. Serve with toasted sourdough.

HARISSA SWEET POTATO & HERB-SPLIT YOGURT

This recipe takes the humble sweet potato and elevates it to a whole new level. Use the best harissa you can find. Some generic brands come sweetened, but the best in my opinion are hot and smoky and require balancing with other ingredients.

....

Serves 4 as a side

4 large sweet potatoes

4 tablespoons harissa

2 tablespoons extra virgin olive oil

150g (5½oz) thick Greek yogurt

salt and freshly ground black pepper

For the quick pickles

2 shallots

1 green chilli

1 quantity Small Batch Master Quick Pickle Liquor (see page 200)

For the green herb sauce

handful of fresh coriander (about 10g/¼oz)

handful of mint, leaves picked (about 10g/¼oz)

handful of flat leaf parsley (about 10g/¼oz)

1 small garlic clove, peeled

1 teaspoon ground cumin

½ teaspoon chilli flakes

4 tablespoons good-quality extra virgin olive oil

juice of 1 lemon

flaky sea salt and freshly ground black pepper

1. Start by making the quick pickles. Slice the shallots and green chilli very thinly into rounds, using a mandolin if you have one. Add to a bowl with the pickle liquor, stir, then set aside.

2. Preheat the oven to 220°C (200°C fan, 425°F), Gas Mark 7.

3. Cut the sweet potatoes into quarters and lay out the wedges on a baking tray. Mix together the harissa, extra virgin olive oil and some salt and pepper in a small bowl, then add half the mixture to the sweet potatoes (saving the other half for later) and toss with your hands until they are well coated. Roast for 30 minutes, turning halfway through, until caramelized on the outside and soft in the middle.

4. Meanwhile, blitz together all the herb sauce ingredients in a blender or food processor until smooth.

5. Remove the baking tray from the oven, add the remaining harissa mixture to the warm sweet potatoes and toss to coat.

6. Spoon the yogurt on to a serving platter, then dollop over the green herb sauce and ripple it through the yogurt. Pile the roasted sweet potatoes on top and finish with the pickled shallots and green chilli. Serve warm.

CRISPY BOMBAY CAULIFLOWER

My dad, who is no great food inspiration for me (sorry, Dad), always seemed to have Bombay mix in his house when I was growing up. I find it incredibly moreish, like most crispy things, and will happily eat an entire bag in one sitting. Consequently, I've always wanted to use it as a garnish in our restaurants, but we've not yet found the right vehicle for it. So when it came to writing this book, I knew I had to include my beloved Bombay mix in a recipe. Cauliflower when deeply roasted has such a complex flavour, so do your best to get that colour, as it will make a huge difference to the end result. This dish is really about the cauliflower and tart yogurt combination; everything else just adds to the fun.

Serves 4 as a side

1 large cauliflower

5 tablespoons olive oil

1 teaspoon ground cumin

1 teaspoon ground coriander

flaky sea salt

a few grinds of black pepper

To serve

150g (5½oz) natural yogurt

1 quantity Green Herb Sauce (see page 91)

50g (1¾oz) Bombay mix, crushed

pinch of chilli powder

small handful of fresh coriander leaves

squeeze of lemon juice

1. Preheat the oven to 240°C (220°C fan, 475°F), Gas Mark 9.

2. Cut the cauliflower into quarters to make 4 wedges, reserving any leaves.

3. Heat 4 tablespoons of the olive oil in a large ovenproof frying pan over a high heat, and fry the cauliflower quarters, cut-sides down, for 3–4 minutes on each flat side, or until they start to colour.

4. Add the cumin, ground coriander, a generous pinch of flaky salt and a few grinds of black pepper to the cauliflower and toss to coat, then place the pan in the oven to cook for 15–20 minutes, depending on the size of the cauliflower, until tender.

5. Place the cauliflower leaves in a bowl and toss in the remaining 1 tablespoon of olive oil. Add the leaves to the pan in the oven for the final 5 minutes of cooking until starting to crisp and char. Remove the pan from the oven and season the leaves with salt.

6. Spoon the yogurt on to a serving platter, then dollop over the green herb sauce and ripple it through the yogurt. Arrange the roasted cauliflower and crispy leaves on top. Sprinkle over the crushed Bombay mix, chilli powder and fresh coriander leaves, and add a squeeze of lemon juice to finish.

MISO MAPLE ONIONS

Another use for our signature miso maple combo. Served over rice or with anything from roast chicken or a piece of fish to bangers and mash, these onions will undoubtedly be the star of the show. Make loads, as they keep well in the fridge for up to a week.

Serves 4 as a side

6 onions

1 quantity Miso Maple Dressing (see page 199)

small handful of thyme leaves, to garnish

1. Preheat the oven to 200°C (180°C fan, 400°F), Gas Mark 6.

2. Peel the onions, then cut them in half and trim off any hairy bits at the root. Place them in a small roasting tray, cut-sides down, so that they fit snuggly together in a single layer.

3. Pour the miso maple dressing over the onions. Roast for 20 minutes, then baste with the marinade, adding 4 tablespoons of water as it starts to caramelize at the bottom. Roast for another 20 minutes, then turn the onions over, cut-sides up, baste again and roast for a final 10 minutes (50 minutes in total).

4. Remove from the oven, then spoon the onions on to a plate, leaving you with a glossy caramel-like gravy at the bottom of the tray. If you have a gas hob, place the tray over a medium flame and add another 4 tablespoons of water. Scrape the sticky bits from all over the tray, stir into the water and gently bubble for a minute until thick and glossy, then turn off the heat. If you don't have a gas hob, simply add the water to the tray and place back in the oven for 2–3 minutes, then remove and stir to get as much of the sticky goodness off the bottom of the pan.

5. Finish by pouring the miso maple onion gravy all over the onions and garnish with the thyme leaves.

AUBERGINE & PRESERVED LEMON

This is a beautiful salad that can be used as part of a mezze (see pages 166–9) or bulked out with a jar of butter beans to make a complete meal. When writing this recipe, I was constantly cooking just about anything that would go well with preserved lemon – stews, beans, salads and dressings. Like anything fermented, it adds a layer of depth and unique acidity that can only be created over time. A great product to have stocked in your larder, and once you acquire the taste, you will become addicted to it, like me.

....

Serves 4 as a side

2 aubergines

2 tablespoons olive oil

½ small red onion, finely sliced

1 red chilli, finely sliced

1 tablespoon capers, plus
1 tablespoon of brine from the jar

½ preserved lemon, finely diced

1 tablespoon chopped dill

1 tablespoon chopped flat leaf
parsley

1 tablespoon chopped chives

2–3 tablespoons good-quality
extra virgin olive oil

salt and freshly ground black pepper

1. Preheat the oven to 240°C (220°C fan, 475°F), Gas Mark 9.

2. Cut the aubergines into 3-cm (1¼-inch) chunks, then place in a bowl with the olive oil and a big pinch of salt and toss until the aubergines are coated in the oil and salt on all sides.

3. Spread the aubergines out in a low-sided roasting tray and roast for 25 minutes, turning them halfway through.

4. Once the aubergines are cooked, add to a large platter or salad bowl, then add the onion, chilli, capers and their brine, preserved lemon and the chopped herbs. Drizzle over the extra virgin olive oil and a good grinding of black pepper and toss to coat.

SPICY BLOOD ORANGE HONEY & CHARRED CARROT

When blood oranges are in season, do use them. Here they feature in the main event of the dish – the flavoured honey. Every time I've made this recipe, I've been left with leftovers of the honey, but that's never been an issue! I love using it for a savoury breakfast with yogurt and nuts, smeared on toast with a soft cheese or in a salad dressing for a unique sweetness.

....

Serves 4 as a side

100g (3½oz) raw skin-on hazelnuts

1 bunch of baby carrots (about 500g/1lb 2oz), or 5–6 regular carrots, scrubbed

2 tablespoons olive oil

2–3 spring onions, finely sliced diagonally

150g (5½oz) soft goats' cheese (I use St Tola)

salt

For the blood orange honey

1 blood orange

olive oil, for drizzling

2 red chillies, skin pierced with a sharp knife

6 garlic cloves, peeled and left whole

300ml (10fl oz) honey

2 rosemary sprigs

To serve

a few fresh coriander sprigs

juice of ½ lime

extra virgin olive oil

flaky sea salt

1. Start by preparing the hazelnuts. Preheat the oven to 200°C (180°C fan, 400°F), Gas Mark 6. Spread the hazelnuts out on a baking tray and roast for about 8–10 minutes until golden brown. Remove from the oven and allow to cool for 5 minutes, then add the nuts to a clean tea towel and rub them inside the tea towel to remove the skins. Roughly chop the nuts or lightly crush using a pestle and mortar, then set aside.

2. For the blood orange honey, first finely grate the zest from the orange and set this aside for later, then cut the orange in half. Heat a griddle pan over a high heat. Drizzle olive oil all over the chillies, garlic and orange halves. Once the pan is scorching hot, add the garlic and chillies to the pan and char for about 4 minutes on each side until blackened. At the same time, place the orange halves, cut-sides down, in the hot pan and char for about 5 minutes until deliciously caramelized and syrupy on the edges.

3. Decant the honey into a saucepan, then place the charred oranges, cut-sides down, in the honey along with the chillies, garlic and rosemary sprigs. Bring the honey to a simmer, then turn the heat off and set aside to infuse. Squeeze all the juice from the oranges into the honey and set aside the gooey sweet chillies and garlic to use later on top of the salad. Strain the honey into an airtight jar and seal. You now have a spicy liquid gold for many occasions!

4. Reheat the griddle pan over a high heat (if your griddle is not ovenproof, use an ovenproof frying pan here instead). Preheat the oven to 200°C (180°C fan, 400°F), Gas Mark 6. Keep the baby carrots whole, but if using regular carrots, cut them into quarters lengthways. Toss the carrots with the olive oil and a good pinch of salt in a bowl. Once the pan is scorching hot, add the carrots and char for about 3–4 minutes on each side, then transfer the pan to the oven for 8–10 minutes or until the carrots are tender.

5. To assemble, arrange the charred carrots and sliced spring onions on a serving plate, then spoon little dollops of the goats' cheese and the roasted hazelnuts around. Slice up the chillies and garlic and scatter those on the plate. Drizzle the blood orange honey generously over everything, and finish with the coriander, blood orange zest and lime juice. Add a sprinkling of flaky sea salt and a splash of extra virgin olive oil and enjoy yourself!

MADE
MOSTLY OF
PLANTS

AUBERGINE MASH & MISO TOFU STEAK

I've never been in love with baba ghanoush, as I find that the smokiness overpowers everything. But a gooey roasted aubergine mashed with a touch of garlic and a drizzle of olive oil is delicious to me. Sometimes I'll top the mash with a piece of white fish steamed in Shaoxing wine, garlic and ginger for a light but special meal. As an alternative, this tofu steak is a comforting plant-based idea and has a baby food mouthfeel with a hint of elegance. Serve alongside a bowl of steamed jasmine rice, and pickled cucumber (see page 201) or a fresh salad such as the Tiger Salad on page 27.

Serves 2

250g (9oz) block of extra-firm tofu

1 quantity Miso Maple Marinade (see page 199)

1 aubergine

2 tablespoons olive oil

½ garlic clove, finely grated

1 tablespoon extra virgin olive oil

1 tablespoon sunflower oil

juice of ½ lemon

1 heaped tablespoon finely chopped chives

salt

1. Put the tofu in a small container, pour over the miso maple marinade and set aside to marinate for at least 10 minutes, or overnight in the fridge if you can.

2. Preheat the oven to 210°C (190°C fan, 410°F), Gas Mark 6½.

3. Slice the aubergine in half lengthways and score the cut sides in a crisscross pattern. Pour 1 tablespoon of the olive oil over each half with a good pinch of salt. Place, cut-sides down, on a baking tray and roast for 25 minutes until soft and caramelized.

4. Remove from the oven, transfer the aubergine to a chopping board and coarsely chop until you have a rough mashed texture. Scoop into a bowl, add the garlic and extra virgin olive oil and mix together.

5. Heat a medium nonstick frying pan over a medium heat. Once hot, add the sunflower oil and then the tofu, leaving behind the excess marinade in the container for now. Fry for 2–3 minutes on the underside until charred and deeply golden. Flip over and fry for another minute, then turn down the heat to low, add the marinade from the container and heat until bubbling. Baste the tofu for a further 2 minutes until the marinade is slightly reduced and caramelized.

6. Remove from the heat and lift the tofu on to the aubergine mash. Spoon over the caramelized miso marinade, then add the chives on top and squeeze over the lemon juice.

'CRISPY' DUKKAH-SPICED CHICKPEAS WITH TOMATO SALAD & YOGURT

I took a food trip to Israel recently and I can't tell you the number of times I was served a dish with a base of yogurt and tahini. Once the vegetable juices seep in, you are left with a delicious sauce that is best mopped up with challah bread. I always have a can of chickpeas in the cupboard, and frying them in oil until crispy is a great way to use them. Make this salad with or without the dukkah. And feel free to use alternative vegetables depending on the season.

Serves 2 as a main, 4 as a side

½ cucumber

150g (5½oz) any in-season tomatoes you can get

handful of Kalamata olives, pitted

1 green chilli, finely sliced

2 tablespoons extra virgin olive oil

finely grated zest and juice of ½ lemon

400g (14oz) can chickpeas, drained

about 150ml (5fl oz) neutral oil, such as vegetable or sunflower

small handful of dill, leaves picked and roughly chopped

small handful of flat leaf parsley, leaves picked and roughly chopped

small handful of chives, roughly chopped

1 garlic clove, finely grated

150g (5½oz) thick Greek yogurt

3 tablespoons tahini

salt and freshly ground black pepper

challah bread, to serve

For the hazelnut dukkah

100g (3½oz) blanched hazelnuts

50g (1¾oz) pumpkin seeds

3 tablespoons sesame seeds

1 teaspoon cumin seeds

1 teaspoon fennel seeds

1 teaspoon coriander seeds

2 teaspoons dried thyme

1. Start by preparing the dukkah. Preheat the oven to 200°C (180°C fan, 400°F), Gas Mark 6.

2. Spread out all the dukkah ingredients except the thyme on a baking tray and roast for 8–10 minutes until the nuts are lightly golden and the spices are fragrant but not burned. Remove from the oven and pour on to a cold tray to stop the ingredients cooking any further, then leave to cool for 10 minutes. Once cooled and the hazelnuts are nice and crunchy, add to a blender with the thyme and pulse a few times until you have a very loose crumb. I like it to be quite chunky, so don't pulse too many times. Season with a pinch of salt and a few grinds of black pepper.

3. Cut the cucumber in half lengthways, scoop out the seedy insides with a spoon and discard, then roughly chop the cucumber into small pieces. Roughly chop the tomatoes into 2-cm (¾-inch) chunks. Add both to a bowl with the olives, green chilli, a generous pinch of salt, the extra virgin olive oil and lemon zest, then set aside.

4. Lay the drained chickpeas out on a clean tea towel or kitchen paper and shake the tea towel or paper to dry, gently rubbing the tops to remove any moisture. The drier the chickpeas, the better this will work and the less the oil will splatter everywhere.

5. Line a tray with kitchen paper. Pour enough of the neutral oil into a medium saucepan to come 2–3cm (¾–1¼ inches) up the pan. Place the pan over a medium-high heat and heat up slightly, then add the chickpeas, swirling them into the oil. Fry for 8–10 minutes until the chickpeas are lightly golden, crisp and light. Scoop them out of the oil on to the paper-lined tray, then toss with 4–5 tablespoons of the dukkah to coat the crispy chickpeas. (The remaining dukkah will keep in an airtight jar for a few weeks.)

6. Toss the chopped herbs into the tomato and cucumber salad with the lemon juice and another pinch of salt.

7. Mix the garlic into the yogurt, then dollop on to individual serving plates or a platter along with the tahini, followed by the tomato and cucumber salad. Top with the dukkah chickpeas. Serve with slices of challah bread.

COLD KIMCHI NOODLES

There are lots of good kimchi brands available now, my preference being the Irish brand and Korean-owned Jaru. Unless you are making stir-fried noodles or serving them in a broth, they are hard to deliver hot, so intentionally serving them cold avoids any disappointment – and they are deliciously refreshing on a warm day.

Serves 4

½ cucumber

300g (10½oz) ramen-style noodles or soba noodles

4 heaped tablespoons kimchi, drained, plus 1 tablespoon of the liquid reserved for the dressing (optional)

2 tablespoons white sesame seeds

vegetable or sunflower oil, for frying

4 eggs

salt

For the gochujang dressing

2 tablespoons sunflower or sesame oil

1 tablespoon reserved kimchi liquid (see above; optional)

1 tablespoon gochujang

1 tablespoon rice vinegar

1 tablespoon soy sauce

1 garlic clove, finely grated

1. Finely slice the cucumber into long matchsticks.

2. Mix all the dressing ingredients together in a small bowl.

3. Cook the noodles in boiling water according to the packet instructions. Scoop out 2 tablespoons of the cooking water into the dressing, then drain the noodles and rinse under cold running water until completely cooled.

4. Drain the noodles well, add to a bowl with the dressing and toss so that the noodles are glossy and red, then divide into 4 serving bowls. Top with the sliced cucumber, a pile of kimchi and the sesame seeds.

5. Add a splash of oil to coat the base of a cast-iron pan and place over a high heat. Crack the eggs into the pan (you may need to do this in batches) and cook for 10 seconds – they should bubble aggressively – then reduce the heat to low to finish cooking them to your liking. The eggs should become crispy and unstick themselves from the pan towards the end of the cooking time.

6. Season the crispy fried eggs with a pinch of salt, then place on top of each bowl to serve.

MISO BUTTER BEAN MASH
WITH SAUTÉED LEEKS & CRISPY AROMATICS

While I was testing this recipe, my mum decided to call by my apartment where she proceeded to stay for three cups of tea and chatted for about two hours. Mum loved the beans and was very complimentary – she's not that difficult to please, at least when it comes to food. This idea combines echoes of different cuisines all in one bowl: umami miso, creamy butter beans and sweet leeks all topped with crispy ginger, garlic and leek tops, that are particularly delicious and have a sort of Tayto cheese and onion crisp flavour to them. It makes for a comforting midweek dish, or a just as special Saturday night dinner!

Serves 2

3 leeks

thumb-sized piece of fresh root ginger

3 garlic cloves

150ml (5fl oz) olive oil

2 x 540g (1lb 3oz) jars butter beans (800g/1lb 12oz drained weight in total)

1½ tablespoons white miso paste

1 tablespoon oyster sauce

juice of 1 lemon

flaky sea salt

1. Slice off the tough green tops of the leeks, but don't discard them, as we're going to make them crispy. Very finely slice the leek tops. Peel the ginger and garlic, then finely slice them into matchsticks about the same size as the leek tops.

2. Pour the olive oil into a small saucepan, add the leek tops and ginger to the cold oil and place over a high heat. Once everything starts to sizzle, fry for 4–6 minutes, or until some of the leeks are beginning to colour, keeping an eye out to ensure they don't burn, and stirring occasionally. Then add the garlic and cook for another 1–2 minutes until everything is lightly golden. Lift out with a slotted spoon on to kitchen paper to crisp up, then season with flaky sea salt, reserving the flavoured cooking oil.

3. Slice the white parts of the leeks into rounds about 2cm (¾ inch) thick and thoroughly wash and dry them. Add the leek rounds along with 4 tablespoons of the reserved flavoured oil to a wide frying pan and season with salt. Stir and then cook over a medium-low heat for about 20 minutes, or until really soft and a little golden on the outside, stirring every so often.

4. While the leeks are cooking, add the butter beans with their liquid and miso to a medium saucepan and heat over a medium heat for about 5 minutes to soften. Once hot and bubbling, turn off the heat, add the oyster sauce and roughly mash the beans to thicken the sauce.

5. Spoon the mashed beans on to a serving plate, top with the sautéed leeks and any of the juices from the pan along with a tablespoon of the flavoured oil, then squeeze over the lemon juice. Finish with the crispy leek tops, ginger and garlic.

THAI CRISPY SALAD

This recipe is inspired by the crispy rice salad at Night + Market, a Thai restaurant in Los Angeles that is like Disneyland to me. Each of their dishes is so spicy, heavily seasoned and intense, it's food that's hard to forget. Their salad is made by deep-frying leftover jasmine rice in curry paste and cornflour, and while delicious, it's a bit laborious and messy to make. So, I've skipped the crispy rice element and used peanuts and lime leaves to bring crunch instead. If you want to turn this into a full meal, I think a retro can of Spam, chopped and pan-fried, is an amazing addition, though I know it divides opinion so you can also add a simple crispy fried egg instead. This dish is everything I love in a salad – sweet, spicy, aromatic, raw, herby and citrusy.

Serves 4 as a side

180g (6¼oz) coarse bulgur wheat

180ml (6¼fl oz) boiling water

2–3 tablespoons Fried Peanuts & Crispy Lime Leaves (see page 196)

½ red onion, finely sliced into half-moons

2 spring onions, finely sliced into thin strips

2-cm (¾-inch) piece of fresh root ginger, peeled and finely sliced into matchsticks

small handful of fresh coriander

lime wedges, to serve

For the fish sauce & chilli-garlic dressing

2 tablespoons fish sauce

juice of 2 limes

2 bird's-eye chillies, very finely sliced into rounds

2 garlic cloves, finely grated

1 teaspoon palm sugar
or 1 tablespoon maple syrup

1. Put the bulgur wheat in a heatproof bowl and pour over the boiling water. Cover with clingfilm or a plate so that it's tightly covered and set aside to soak for 20 minutes.

2. Uncover the bulgur wheat and separate the grains with a fork.

3. Mix all the dressing ingredients together in a small bowl.

4. Add the bulgur, a handful of the fried peanuts and lime leaves to a salad bowl. Next, add half the red onion, spring onions, ginger and coriander, then add all the dressing and toss together so that everything is coated in the dressing.

5. Top with the remaining fried peanuts and lime leaves, onions, ginger and coriander and serve immediately with lime wedges on the side. Your mouth should explode with spicy, aromatic and salty notes bouncing all over the plate!

UMAMI KNOWS BEST

This plant-based salad is a mainstay on our menu and it's what Jack and I call a 'complete salad'. It's got loads of elements that complement each other and will keep you interested right down to the last bite. Now I know that in consequence this all looks a bit daunting, but the processes are simple and you need not prepare all the elements – if you made only the miso mushrooms, you would be all the happier for that. The ginger sesame dressing is the most addictive component, and makes eating a full bowl of kale surprisingly delightful! It's made with both fresh and pickled ginger, creating a fragrant, sweet and sharp sauce that you will have little trouble using up.

Serves 4

200g (7oz) curly kale, stalks removed and leaves finely shredded

¼ red cabbage, finely shredded

4 spring onions, finely sliced

1–2 red chillies, finely sliced

1 quantity Pickled Carrots & Bean Sprouts (see page 201)

1 quantity Miso Shrooms (see page 114)

1 quantity Spicy Tofu (see page 114)

For the ginger sesame dressing

100g (3½oz) pickled ginger

2-cm (¾-inch) piece of fresh root ginger, peeled and roughly chopped

2 garlic cloves, peeled

juice of 1 lemon

4 tablespoons olive oil

2 tablespoons tahini

2 tablespoons maple syrup

1 tablespoon soy sauce

1 tablespoon water

1 teaspoon sesame oil

pinch of salt

To serve

cooked brown rice

1 quantity Peanut Sesame Brittle (see page 114)

1. Blitz all the dressing ingredients together in a blender– ideally in a high-speed blender for a fully emulsified result – until smooth and creamy.

2. Mix the kale, red cabbage, pickled carrots and bean sprouts, spring onions, chillies, the miso shrooms, spicy tofu and brown rice in a large bowl and toss together.

3. Pour over the dressing and toss with your hands so that everything is completely coated.

4. Serve in individual bowls and top with 1–2 tablespoons of the peanut sesame brittle.

MISO SHROOMS

250g (9oz) portobello mushrooms

1 quantity Miso Maple Marinade (see page 199)

1. Preheat the oven to 210°C (190°C fan, 410°F), Gas Mark 6.
2. Cut the mushrooms into slices about 5mm (¼ inch) thick. Place in a low-sided roasting tray, pour over 4 tablespoons of the marinade and toss until all the mushroom slices are nicely coated. Roast for 25 minutes until they are really crispy and golden. Scape all the sticky goodness from the bottom of the tray and stir back into the mushrooms along with the remaining marinade to glaze them further.

SPICY TOFU

2 tablespoons sunflower oil

2 tablespoons soy sauce

1 tablespoon rice vinegar

1 tablespoon white miso paste

1 tablespoon maple syrup

1 teaspoon cayenne pepper

2 garlic cloves, finely grated

200g (7oz) extra-firm tofu

1. Preheat the oven to 210°C (190°C fan, 410°F), Gas Mark 6.
2. Line a baking tray with nonstick baking paper.
3. Mix the sunflower oil, soy sauce, rice vinegar, miso paste, maple syrup, cayenne pepper and garlic in a small bowl until well combined.
4. Cut the tofu into 2-cm (¾-inch) cubes. Place on the lined tray, add half the marinade (saving the other half to glaze and dress the tofu afterwards) and toss until well coated. Bake for 20–25 minutes. Remove from the oven and toss in the remaining marinade to glaze.

PEANUT SESAME BRITTLE

225g (8oz) roasted, unsalted skinned peanuts

3 tablespoons olive oil

3 tablespoons maple syrup

2 tablespoons mixed white and black sesame seeds

½ teaspoon cayenne pepper

½ teaspoon chilli flakes

large pinch of flaky sea salt

1. Preheat the oven to 210°C (190°C fan, 410°F), Gas Mark 6.
2. Line a small, low-sided roasting tray with nonstick baking paper.
3. Mix all the ingredients together in a bowl, then pour into the lined tray and spread out. You should have a good layer of the liquid at the bottom here, so if you don't, just top it up with a bit more oil and maple syrup. You want the peanuts to fry and caramelize in the liquid. Bake for 8–10 minutes until lightly golden and you have a bubbling caramel. Remove from the oven and set aside for the peanut mixture to cool completely in the tray.
4. Once cooled, lift the brittle off the tray and peel off the lining paper. Break the brittle into little clusters. Any left over can be stored in an airtight container for up to 2 months.

GOCHUJANG BOWL

A salad that has cult status, this is one that our customers regularly ask us to bring back (pictured overleaf). Gochujang is a wonderful spicy, umami Korean fermented chilli paste, used in both the hot dressing and the spicy cashews which are the star of the show – sticky, spicy and a little messy (which is ultimately why we had to take them off our menu), but they're a lot of fun if you are serving a small group. To make this dish vegetarian, replace the chicken with the spicy tofu on page 114.

Serves 4–6

8 bone-in, skin-on chicken thighs

2 aubergines

generous pinch of salt

2 tablespoons sunflower oil

2 tablespoons runny honey

1 tablespoon white sesame seeds

200g (7oz) udon noodles

1 quantity Gochujang Dressing (see page 106)

200g (7oz) curly kale, stalks removed and shredded

½ quantity Pickled Red Cabbage (see page 201)

1 quantity Gochujang Cashews (see page 117)

For the ginger & chilli marinade

4 garlic cloves, finely grated

3-cm (1¼-inch) piece of fresh root ginger, peeled and finely grated

finely grated zest of 1 lime

2 tablespoons sunflower oil

1 teaspoon Korean chilli flakes (or regular chilli flakes if you don't have them)

generous pinch of flaky sea salt

To serve

4 spring onions, finely sliced

1 green chilli, finely sliced

small handful of mint, leaves picked

finely grated zest and juice of 1 lime

1. Start by marinating the chicken. Mix all the marinade ingredients together in a medium bowl. Add the chicken thighs and rub the marinade into them with your hands, making sure they're all nicely coated. Cover and leave to marinate in the fridge for up to 24 hours, but if you don't have time then it's fine to skip this.

2. Preheat the oven to 220°C (200°C fan, 425°F), Gas Mark 7.

3. Place the chicken thighs, skin-side down, in an ovenproof frying pan over a medium heat and fry for 4–6 minutes until the skin is lightly golden, then flip over, transfer the pan to the oven and cook for 35–40 minutes until well browned and cooked through.

4. While the chicken is in the oven, slice the aubergines into rounds 2cm (¾ inch) thick. Lay out in a low-sided roasting tray, sprinkle with the salt and sunflower oil and toss to coat. Drizzle each aubergine round with an equal quantity of the honey and then sprinkle with the sesame seeds so that you have a nice layer on each. Place in the oven with the chicken and roast for 25 minutes until softened and the sesame seeds are golden and crisp on top.

5. Once cooked, remove the chicken from the oven and leave to rest in the pan for 10 minutes. Pick the chicken off the bones and shred, leaving the meat in the pan to toss in the juices.

6. Cook the udon noodles according to the packet instructions, then drain and rinse under cold running water until completely cooled.

7. When ready to serve, pour some of the warmed gochujang dressing over the kale in a large bowl and scrunch it with your hands so that it wilts a little.

8. Add the shredded chicken to the kale, along with the noodles, aubergines, pickled red cabbage, spring onions, green chilli and mint. Squeeze over the lime juice and add the remaining dressing, then toss everything gently. Serve in individual bowls and top with the gochujang cashews.

GOCHUJANG CASHEWS

2 tablespoons gochujang

1 tablespoon honey

1 tablespoon soy sauce

1 tablespoon sunflower oil

1 teaspoon Korean chilli flakes
or chilli powder

200g (7oz) raw unsalted cashew
nuts

1. Preheat the oven to 200°C
   (180°C fan, 400°F), Gas Mark 6.
   Line a low-sided baking tray
   with nonstick baking paper.

2. Mix together all the
   ingredients except the
   cashews in a bowl, then stir in
   the cashews until each one is
   completely coated in the sauce.

3. Tip on to the lined tray and
   spread out in a single layer.
   Bake for about 8 minutes until
   golden and bubbling.

4. Remove from the oven and set
   aside for the cashew mixture
   to cool completely in the tray.
   Once cooled, break them up a
   little. They are supposed to be
   a little chewy and sticky rather
   than crunchy.

GOCHUJANG DRESSING

4 tablespoons sunflower oil

2 tablespoons rice vinegar

2 tablespoons gochujang

1 tablespoon soy sauce

1 tablespoon fish sauce

1. Put all the dressing
   ingredients in a small
   saucepan and whisk together.
   Place over a medium heat for
   about a minute until warmed
   and infused.

WHITE BEANS, BLISTERED TOMATOES & AIOLI

This one has very little preparation involved. I've even given you the option of skipping the homemade aioli (see my cheat below – it will still be delicious). I use the technique of blistering tomatoes all the time, as it's so easy and versatile depending on what you're feeling like cooking up, whether it be a salad, pasta, fish or beans. A great quick dish for a bright evening.

Serves 2

1 lemon

400g (14oz) cherry tomatoes

3 tablespoons olive oil

1 tablespoon fennel seeds

1 tablespoon runny honey

pinch of flaky sea salt

540g (1lb 3oz) jar white beans, drained (400g/14oz drained weight)

For the aioli (optional)

1 egg yolk

about 1 tablespoon lemon juice

1 teaspoon Dijon mustard

2 garlic cloves, finely grated

250ml (9fl oz) olive oil, plus extra for drizzling

salt

For the rocket salad (optional)

100g (3½oz) rocket

small handful of oregano (about 10g/¼oz), leaves picked

juice of ½ lemon

pinch of salt

1. Preheat the oven to 220°C (200°C fan, 425°F), Gas Mark 7.

2. Peel the zest from the lemon with a peeler and add it to a small roasting tray with the tomatoes, olive oil, fennel seeds, honey and sea salt. You want the tomatoes to all fit snugly so that they roast evenly together. Roast for 15 minutes until slightly charred and you have a sweet tomato-y caramel at the bottom of the tray.

3. Meanwhile, make the aioli, if using. Add the egg yolk, lemon juice, mustard, garlic and a pinch of salt to a bowl, then whisk together until the mixture combines and emulsifies a little. Very slowly, add the olive oil little by little and then in a steady stream until you have a thick creamy consistency. (Alternatively, cheat by making a garlic mayonnaise by mixing 1 finely grated garlic clove and 1 tablespoon of lemon juice into some shop-bought mayonnaise in a small bowl.)

4. Remove the tray from the oven, add the drained beans and carefully toss them into the tomatoes, then roast for another 10 minutes to allow the flavours to combine.

5. For the salad, if making, add the rocket and oregano to a small bowl, then dress with the lemon juice and salt.

6. Remove the beans and tomatoes from the oven and spoon on to a serving plate. Serve with a dollop of the aioli or garlic mayo drizzled with extra olive oil, and with the salad on the side.

BASIL ORZO WITH RED PEPPER & PINE NUTS

Orzo is like a cross between a long-grain rice and short-cut pasta, and its almost buttery texture works so well through a salad. This tastes even better the next day, so make extra and have it for lunch during the week.

Serves 4

4 red peppers (ideally Romano, but any will work)

2 tablespoons olive oil

50g (1¾oz) pine nuts

1 tablespoon fennel seeds

250g (9oz) orzo pasta

2 handfuls of rocket

salt and freshly ground black pepper

For the basil dressing

large handful of basil (20g/¾oz)

4 tablespoons extra virgin olive oil, plus extra to finish

1 garlic clove, finely grated or very finely chopped

juice of ½ lemon, plus extra to serve

½ tablespoon white wine vinegar

To serve

a chunk of Parmesan cheese, shaved with a vegetable peeler

flaky sea salt

1. Preheat the oven to 220°C (200°C fan, 425°F), Gas Mark 7.

2. Place the peppers in a low-sided roasting tray and drizzle with the olive oil, then season generously with salt. Roast for 20–25 minutes until the skins are blistered and charred slightly.

3. Meanwhile, toast the pine nuts and fennel seeds in a small dry frying pan over a medium heat for 1 minute until lightly golden. Remove from the pan and set aside to cool.

4. Cook the orzo in a pan of salted boiling water for 8 minutes, or according to the packet instructions.

5. While the orzo is cooking, blitz all the dressing ingredients together in a blender, seasoning with a pinch of salt and a few grinds of black pepper, until smooth and bright green. Once the orzo is cooked, drain and rinse under cold running water until completely cooled, then drain well and add it to a bowl.

6. Remove the peppers from the oven and set aside to cool a little, then pull off the tops and remove the seeds and all the skin, and slice the peppers into thin strips.

7. Pour the dressing over the orzo, then toss in the rocket and the roasted peppers. Pile on to a serving plate and top with the toasted pine nuts and fennel seeds, shaved Parmesan, a squeeze of lemon juice, flaky sea salt, black pepper and a little extra virgin olive oil.

SUMMER PASTA SALAD

This recipe is more of a reminder not to forget about pasta salad. Making pasta can be a stressful business: trying to get the sauce the right consistency and judging how much pasta water to add; worrying about serving it hot enough and whether you remembered to warm the serving bowls or plates. And by the time everyone has sat down, it's lost that desirable glossy finish. Pasta salad, however, is altogether less stressful. You can play around with the vegetables here – try adding the blistered tomatoes from the recipe on page 118. It's also easy to make in bulk to use as lunches during the week, or you could be that person who brings a pasta salad to the summer barbecue – everybody's favourite person!

Serves 4

1 aubergine, cut into 2-cm (¾-inch) chunks

1 courgette, cut into 2-cm (¾-inch) chunks

1 fennel bulb, cut into wedges 1cm (½ inch) thick

3 tablespoons olive oil (for roasting the vegetables), plus extra for drizzling

50g (1¾oz) skin-on hazelnuts

1 teaspoon fennel seeds

400g (14oz) farfalle pasta

1 tablespoon finely chopped chives

small handful of basil leaves

3 tablespoons extra virgin olive oil

1 tablespoon white wine vinegar, plus extra to finish

salt and freshly ground black pepper

For the pickled onion

1 red onion, halved and finely sliced into half-moons

juice of ½ lemon

To serve

1 ball of mozzarella cheese

pinch of chilli flakes

1. Preheat the oven to 210°C (190°C fan, 410°F), Gas Mark 6½.

2. Put the aubergine, courgette and fennel in a roasting tray and toss with the olive oil and a pinch of salt. Roast for 25–30 minutes until everything is soft and golden at the edges.

3. Spread the hazelnuts and fennel seeds out on a baking tray, place in the oven with the veg and roast for 8 minutes until lightly golden. Remove from the oven and set aside to cool.

4. While the veg finishes roasting, cook the pasta in a large pan of salted boiling water according to the packet instructions, then drain and rinse under cold running water until completely cooled. Drain well and add to a bowl with a generous drizzle of olive oil to coat.

5. Remove the roasted veg from the oven. Roughly chop the fennel into bite-sized pieces, then toss with the pasta as soon as you can so that it doesn't stick together.

6. For the pickled onion, place the red onion in a small bowl, squeeze over the lemon juice and add a pinch of salt. Scrunch the onion together with your hands so that it's coated in the lemon juice and starts to turn bright pink.

7. Toss the herbs, pickled onion, extra virgin olive oil, vinegar, a pinch of salt and a few grinds of black pepper into the pasta.

8. Transfer to a serving platter, tear over the mozzarella and crush the fennel-y hazelnuts on top, adding the chilli flakes and a final drizzle of extra virgin oilve oil to finish.

GREEN COCONUT RICE

This recipe was co-developed together with my very talented friend, Kitty. It really is a combination of all my favourite ingredients: I have rice with nearly every meal, fresh coriander is my number one herb, and I put green chillies and spring onions on everything! The crispy curry leaf cashew topping makes most things better.

....

Serves 4

300g (10½oz) jasmine rice

1 bunch of fresh coriander (about 30g/1oz)

125ml (4fl oz) water

175ml (6fl oz) full-fat coconut milk (if using canned, shake before opening)

2 bunches of spring onions (about 12–14), trimmed but left whole

3–4 green chillies

4 tablespoons olive oil

finely grated zest and juice of 2 limes, plus extra zest to finish

salt and freshly ground black pepper

For the crispy curry leaf cashews

80g (3oz) raw unsalted cashew nuts

2 tablespoons olive oil

generous handful of fresh curry leaves

To serve

150g (5½oz) natural yogurt

½ teaspoon ground cumin

1. Wash the rice until the water runs clear, then drain and add it to a medium saucepan with a lid. Blitz the fresh coriander in a blender with the water until it is a completely smooth green liquid. Add this to the rice pan along with the coconut milk and a pinch of salt and stir together so that the rice is evenly distributed and green.

2. Bring to the boil, then cover the pan with the lid, immediately turn the heat down to its lowest setting (you want it to be very lightly bubbling, but not boiling or simmering) and cook for 15–20 minutes. Check the rice has cooked by tasting a grain; once it's tender, turn the heat off and fluff the rice up with a fork. Place the lid back on and leave to steam for 5 minutes.

3. Once the rice is cooking, prepare the crispy curry leaf cashews. Preheat the oven to 200°C (180°C fan, 400°F), Gas Mark 6.

4. Toss the cashews in 1 tablespoon of the olive oil and a pinch of salt in a bowl. Spread out on a baking tray and roast for 6 minutes until beginning to turn golden. In the same bowl, add the curry leaves, remaining oil and a pinch of salt and toss, then add them to the tray with the cashews and roast for 2 minutes. Remove from the oven and set aside to cool and turn crispy.

5. Heat a large dry frying pan over a high heat. Once smoking hot, add the spring onions and green chillies, in batches, and cook for a few minutes until charred on all sides and soft inside. Once they are all ready, add them back to the smoking hot pan with a pinch of salt and 2 teaspoons of water. The water will instantly bubble away and evaporate after a minute or so. Once the water has gone, turn off the heat and tip the spring onions and green chillies into a bowl. (Fill the pan up with water at this point to help the cleaning process!)

6. Mix together the olive oil, lime zest and juice and a pinch of salt and pepper in a small bowl for the dressing, then add half to the charred spring onions and green chillies and toss to coat.

7. Once the rice has finished steaming, add the second half of the dressing and stir so that the rice is well coated.

8. Tip the dressed rice on to a serving plate, followed by a few big dollops of the yogurt. Now pile on the charred spring onions and green chillies with any dressing that has pooled in the bowl. Finish with the roasted cashews and curry leaves and a little more lime zest, and sprinkle the cumin over the yogurt.

TUTTS'S 'CRISPY' PILAU RICE

This recipe comes from the Sprout test kitchen and was developed by our executive chef who has been with us since day one, Tutts. It's another idea that for one reason or another couldn't be launched in our restaurants, but wow is it delicious! The rice is cooked in a pilau-style base seasoning, then combined with sweet caramelized onions, lots of herbs and spicy peanuts. It makes an amazing addition to an Indian-themed meal, or serve Middle Eastern style with cooked lentils and natural yogurt for some quality comfort food. You can cheat a bit here and buy a jar of caramelized onions if you don't have time to make them.

Serves 4

250g (9oz) basmati rice

4 tablespoons olive oil

2 onions, diced

3 garlic cloves, very finely chopped

1 cinnamon stick

2 teaspoons cumin seeds

1 teaspoon yellow mustard seeds

1 teaspoon garam masala

1 teaspoon coriander seeds

250ml (9fl oz) vegetable stock or water

small handful of fresh coriander leaves, chopped

small handful of flat leaf parsley leaves, chopped

salt

a few spring onions tops, finely sliced, to garnish

natural yogurt, to serve

For the caramelized onions

6 onions

5 tablespoons olive oil

For the spicy peanuts

150g (5½oz) raw skin-on peanuts

1 teaspoon olive oil

½ teaspoon chilli powder

1. Wash the rice until the water runs clear, then drain. Add the olive oil to a wide pan with a lid along with the diced onions and the garlic and a cartouche (a layer of baking paper covering the surface of the onions). Sweat over a low heat for 10 minutes until the onions have softened but not coloured. Remove the cartouche, stir in all the spices and cook for a further 2 minutes.

2. Add the rice and stock or water to the pan and stir to mix. Bring to the boil, then cover the pan with the lid, immediately turn the heat down to its lowest setting and cook for 15–20 minutes. Remove from the heat, fluff the rice up with a fork, then place the lid back on and leave to steam for 5 minutes.

3. Once the rice is underway, make the caramelized onions. Peel, halve and finely slice the onions into half-moons equal in size, using a mandolin if you have one. Add to a wide sauté pan along with the olive oil and ½ teaspoon of salt, and cook over a medium heat, stirring and scraping the bottom of the pan regularly with a spatula to deglaze, for 22–26 minutes until the onions have reduced. Ensure the onions don't catch or colour as they will become bitter. Once caramelized, the onions should taste amazing and you'll regret not having done more!

4. Meanwhile, for the spicy peanuts, preheat the oven to 200°C (180°C fan, 400°F), Gas Mark 6. Toss the peanuts in the olive oil on a baking tray and season with the chilli powder and salt, then roast for 8–10 minutes until lightly and evenly roasted. Be sure not to overdo it, as a burnt peanut tastes rancid. Remove from the oven and set aside to cool.

5. To assemble, stir the caramelized onions, spicy peanuts and chopped herbs through the rice, then pile on to a large serving platter. Garnish with the spring onion tops and coriander sprigs and serve with a bowl of natural yogurt drizzled with olive oil on the side and allow everybody to help themselves.

SUPER GUACABOWLE

Back in 2015 when Sprout first began, we set out to create a superfood salad that actually tasted delicious rather than feeling like a sacrifice to flavour. The result? An iconic salad that's been on our menu since day one (which is also featured on the cover of this book). Serve the butternut squash warm, and if you feel like bulking it out, warm quinoa is a great addition.

....

Serves 4

1 butternut squash, about 1kg (2lb 4oz)

3 garlic cloves, very finely chopped

1 teaspoon dried mixed herbs

3 tablespoons olive oil, plus 1 teaspoon

50g (1¾oz) mixed seeds

3 avocados

1 bunch of fresh coriander (about 15g/½oz), chopped

juice of 1 lime, plus extra for soaking the apple

1 apple

4 handfuls of seasonal greens

2 carrots, grated

¼ red cabbage, finely shredded

seeds of 1 pomegranate

100g (3½oz) feta cheese, crumbled

1 quantity French dressing (see page 197)

flaky sea salt and freshly ground black pepper

1. Preheat the oven to 220°C (200°C fan, 425°F), Gas Mark 7.

2. Cut the butternut squash in half lengthways and scoop out the seeds, then cut into half-moons about 2cm (¾ inch) thick. Place them on a large baking tray and add the garlic, dried mixed herbs, the 3 tablespoons of olive oil and a generous pinch of salt and pepper, then toss with your hands until well coated. Spread out on the tray, allowing enough space in between the wedges to maximize colour and caramelization, and roast for 25 minutes.

3. Spread the mixed seeds out on a separate baking tray and sprinkle with flaky sea salt and the 1 teaspoon of olive oil. Add to the oven with the squash for 5–10 minutes until lightly toasted.

4. While the squash is roasting, halve, stone and peel the avocados, then roughly chop, keeping the consistency chunky. Mix with the chopped coriander and lime juice in a bowl and season to taste with salt and pepper.

5. Dice the apple, then leave to soak in a bowl of cold water with a squeeze of lime until ready to assemble the salad to stop it from discolouring.

6. Once the squash is ready, transfer to a large bowl and add the drained apple along with all the remaining salad ingredients except the feta. Pour over the dressing and toss together, then serve the salad garnished with the guacamole, toasted seeds and feta.

MEAT & POULTRY SALADS

PAPRIKA CHICA

Our mum lived in Salamanca, western Spain, when she was is in her twenties and fell in love with the language, a Spanish man (who is not my dad) and, of course, the food. Growing up, we spent summer holidays in Spain, searching for little hole-in-the wall amazing tapas bars where Mum encouraged us to try everything. Jack and I owe her a lot for establishing our love of food from an early age. She brought back with her a recipe for a dipping sauce, which in the '90s would have been the height of sophistication, served to us with crudités at family gatherings. We called it 'Mum's Spanish dip' and it's a great way to get kids eating lots of vegetables. In later years, we developed her recipe further and it became Sprout's 'Paprika Yogurt', which has been a bestseller. Thanks, Mum!

....

Serves 4

8 boneless chicken thighs

200g (7oz) brown basmati rice

5 tablespoons olive oil

2 garlic cloves, very finely chopped

5 bay leaves

400ml (14fl oz) water

2 tablespoons white wine

2 sweet potatoes

1 teaspoon chilli flakes

1 quantity French Dressing
(see page 197)

1 quantity Paprika Yogurt
(see page 199)

salt and freshly ground black pepper

For the garlic & herb marinade

3 tablespoons olive oil

3 garlic cloves, very finely chopped

1 heaped tablespoon chopped
fresh sage

1 heaped tablespoon oregano leaves

1 heaped tablespoon thyme leaves

1 heaped tablespoon chopped
rosemary leaves

To serve

4 large handfuls of spinach

5 spring onions, sliced into rounds

2 red chillies, sliced into rounds

1. Start by marinating the chicken. To make the marinade, blitz the olive oil, garlic and herbs in a food processor, then season with a generous pinch of salt and black pepper. Add the marinade to the chicken thighs and rub it in with your hands, making sure the chicken is nicely coated. Cover and leave to marinate at room temperature for at least 30 minutes, but ideally in the fridge for 24 hours.

2. When ready to cook, wash the rice until the water runs clear, then drain. Place the rice in a medium saucepan and add 2 tablespoons of the olive oil, the finely chopped garlic, bay leaves, a big pinch of salt and the water. Bring to the boil, then cover the pan with a tight-fitting lid and immediately turn the heat down to its lowest setting and cook for 40 minutes, or until all the water has been absorbed. Turn the heat off and fluff the rice up with a fork. Place the lid back on and leave to steam for 10 minutes.

3. Once the rice is underway, preheat the oven to 220°C (200°C fan, 425°F), Gas Mark 7.

4. Transfer the marinated chicken to a baking tray, ensuring each thigh has plenty of space to distribute the heat and achieve some colour. Add the white wine to the tray, then roast for 35–45 minutes until well browned and cooked through, but as these are thighs, you can afford to cook them for longer without them becoming dry.

5. Once the chicken is in the oven, cut the sweet potatoes into 2-cm (¾-inch) cubes. Place on a baking tray, add the remaining 3 tablespoons of olive oil, the chilli flakes and a generous pinch of salt, then toss with your hands until well coated. Add to the oven with the chicken and roast for 20–30 minutes until you have some crispy edges and the potatoes are tender.

6. When everything is cooked, remove the chicken from the oven, strip the meat from the bones and slice. Add the roasted chicken to a large mixing bowl together with the sweet potato, brown rice, spinach, sliced spring onions and red chilli. Pour over the dressing and gently toss. Divide into indivual bowls and top with a dollop of the paprika yogurt.

DUCK & ORANGE WITH NAM-JIM-STYLE DRESSING

My mind usually drifts towards South East Asia for inspiration because everything tends to whack with flavour. I call this kind of food 'a smack on the lips'. This was the idea for a twist on the classic combination of duck and orange, with a nam jim-style dressing. Duck breasts release a huge amount of fat when rendering and I always save it to make duck-fat rice, or you could use it for roasting potatoes on another day. When testing and seeing just how much of the fat was left in the pan, and wanting to add more flavour to the salad, I decided to crisp up the herbs in it. They were sensational, like savoury herb duck scratchings! It's just as beautiful with the herbs left in their fresh state in my view, so I'll let you make up your own mind.

....

Serves 4

4 duck breasts

2 oranges of any kind (I like to use blood oranges when in season)

salt

For the orange & chilli dressing

2 garlic cloves, finely grated

thumb-sized piece of fresh root ginger, peeled and finely grated

½ banana shallot, finely diced

1–2 bird's-eye chillies (depending how spicy you like it), finely sliced into rounds

2 teaspoons finely chopped fresh coriander stems

juice of 1 orange

2 tablespoons soy sauce

1 tablespoon rice vinegar

1 tablespoon sunflower oil

For the crispy herbs

handful of Thai basil, leaves picked (15g/½oz)

handful of fresh coriander (15g/½oz)

1. Mix all the dressing ingredients together in a small bowl. Taste for seasoning and set aside.

2. Preheat the oven to 200°C (180°C fan, 400°F), Gas Mark 6.

3. Trim off any excess fat from the duck breasts, but don't throw the fat away! Season each side of the duck with salt, then place in a cold ovenproof frying pan, skin-side down, together with the offcuts of fat. Turn the heat to medium-low and render the fat for about 10 minutes (be patient here, as you need to go low and slow) until you're left with a good layer of melted fat in the pan and the fat on the duck is thin and crisped up. Pour the excess fat into a bowl, then flip the duck over so that it's skin-side up. Transfer the pan to the oven and cook for 6 minutes. (Keep an eye on them, as the duck breasts may take a little less or more time to cook depending on their size.)

4. Remove the duck from the oven and place on a chopping board to rest.

5. If crisping up your herbs, set a sieve over a heatproof bowl and line a plate with kitchen paper. Place the pan back on the hob and heat the duck fat over a medium heat. Carefully add the herbs (they will spit initially, so stand back as you add them to the pan) and cook for 30 seconds, then pour the fat and herbs into the sieve so that the bowl underneath catches the fat, reserving the fat for another day. Place the herbs on the paper-lined plate to cool and season with salt.

6. Slice off the top and bottom of the oranges, then peel the skin off with a sharp serrated knife, removing as much of the white pith as you can. Then slice the oranges into rounds 1cm (½ inch) thick and place on a serving platter. Squeeze any of the remaining juice from the skins into the dressing.

7. Slice the duck up and lay it over the orange slices. Spoon over 4–5 tablespoons of the dressing, then top with the herbs (crispy and fresh) and add more chilli if you like, depending on your heat threshold. Serve immediately.

THE 'SATAYSFIED' CHICKEN

A top seller in our restaurants, this dish may be the reason you bought this book. This isn't exactly how we present it in our restaurants because I thought I'd share a version more suitable to prepare at home. But if you do want to recreate the restaurant version, make the Ginger Sesame Dressing on page 113 and serve with spinach and finely sliced spring onions along with some Pickled Cucumber (see page 201), which is a perfect match for the rich satay sauce, then sprinkle with the Peanut Sesame Brittle from page 114.

....

Serves 4

4 skin-on chicken breasts

3 tablespoons olive oil

4-cm (1½-inch) piece of fresh root ginger, peeled and finely chopped or grated

3 garlic cloves, finely sliced

1 tablespoon Madras curry powder

1 teaspoon ground turmeric

1 red chilli, deseeded and finely chopped

400ml (14oz) can full-fat coconut milk

4 tablespoons crunchy peanut butter

1 teaspoon soy sauce

juice of 1 lime

salt

1 quantity Sweet Pickled Cucumber & Shallot Salad (see page 29)

a few handfuls of Peanut Sesame Brittle (see page 114), to serve

For the coriander & spring onion brown rice

200g (7oz) brown basmati rice

400ml (14fl oz) water

handful of fresh coriander, roughly chopped

4 spring onions, roughly chopped

1. Start by preparing the rice. Wash the rice until the water runs clear, then drain. Add to a medium pan with a lid along with the measured water and a small pinch of salt. Bring to the boil, then cover the pan with the lid, immediately turn the heat down to its lowest setting and cook for 40 minutes, or until all the water has evaporated. Turn the heat off and fluff the rice up with a fork. Place the lid back on and leave to steam for 10 minutes.

2. Meanwhile, season the chicken breasts with salt and 1 tablespoon of the olive oil. Place a large nonstick frying pan over a medium heat, and once hot, add the chicken breasts to the pan, skin-side down, along with another tablespoon of olive oil. Fry for 4–5 minutes until deeply golden and crisp. Flip the chicken over and cook for another 4 minutes until cooked through (the timing may differ depending on the size of your chicken breasts). Remove the chicken from the pan on to a plate to rest.

3. Add the remaining tablespoon of olive oil to the chicken juices in the pan along with the ginger, garlic, curry powder, turmeric and chilli and fry for 2–3 minutes over a medium heat until softened and fragrant. Pour in the coconut milk and bring to a gentle simmer. Then add the peanut butter and stir until the sauce thickens slightly. Turn off the heat and season with the soy sauce. Squeeze in the lime juice and pour in the resting juices that have collected on the bottom of the plate of chicken.

4. Once the rice has cooled a little, toss in the coriander and spring onions and season with more salt if needed.

5. Prepare individual plates or assemble a family-style platter by pouring the satay sauce on to a warmed serving dish, carve the chicken breasts and place on top of the sauce, and scatter over the sweet pickled cucumber and shallot and peanut sesame brittle. Serve with the coriander and spring onion rice on the side.

CHICKEN PHO GA

I love a big screaming hot bowl of pho; it's a Vietnamese aromatic soup that I believe to be life-giving. Boiling a whole chicken is very rewarding, maximizing every ounce of the bird. The classic topping of fresh limey herbs with thinly sliced sweet white onion is my excuse for bringing a soup into a salad cookbook. Use the leftover leg meat for the Shredded Chicken in 'Mala' Sichuan Dressing, on page 142.

....

Serves 4–6

1 free-range or corn-fed chicken, about 1.5kg (3lb 5oz)

2.5 litres (4½ pints) water, or enough to cover the chicken

1 teaspoon fine sea salt

1 large onion, halved

5-cm (2-inch) piece of fresh root ginger, peeled and left whole

5 garlic cloves, peeled and left whole

3 star anise

1 teaspoon fennel seeds

1 teaspoon coriander seeds

1 tablespoon sugar

1 teaspoon MSG (optional)

about 300g (10½oz) flat rice noodles

salt

For the herb salad

generous mix of fresh coriander, Thai basil and picked mint leaves (about 25g/1oz of each)

½ white onion, halved and very finely sliced into half-moons

5-cm (2-inch) chunk of daikon, peeled and sliced into thin matchsticks

To serve

2 bird's-eye chillies, finely sliced into 4 tablespoons fish sauce

hoisin sauce or sriracha

1 lime, cut into wedges

1. Place the chicken in a large pot with a lid, pour over enough water to cover it and add the fine sea salt. Cover the pan with the lid and bring to the boil. Once boiling, remove the lid and rapidly simmer for about 45 minutes, skimming off any impurities that rise to the top, until the skin on the leg meat has split and the chicken is cooked through.

2. While the chicken is poaching, place a dry frying pan over a high heat. Add the onion halves, ginger and garlic and cook for about 10 minutes until charred on all sides. Remove from the pan and set aside.

3. In the same pan, toast the star anise and fennel and coriander seeds for 1 minute until they smell fragrant, then set aside with the charred aromatics.

4. Once the chicken is cooked, carefully transfer it to a dish to catch all the juices. Allow to rest and cool for at least 10 minutes. Slice the breasts off the chicken with a paring knife (or just pull off with kitchen tongs for a less polished look), pick the leg and wing meat off the bones and season with salt while it's warm. Allow the dark meat to cool and save for another recipe (see overleaf, for example). Add all the stripped bones and carcass back to the pot with the broth.

5. You can take the pot of broth in any direction of flavour. I sometimes reserve half as a plain chicken stock to keep in the fridge to use during the week. Add the charred aromatics, toasted spices, sugar and MSG, if using, to the broth with another pinch of salt, and bring to a simmer until you're happy with the flavour. This can be anything from 30 minutes to 2 hours, depending on how much patience you have. Pour through a fine sieve set over a large bowl to remove the spices and aromatics for a beautifully pure-tasting broth.

6. While the broth is simmering, toss the herb salad ingredients together in a large bowl. Set aside until serving.

7. When you're ready to serve, cook the noodles according to the packet instructions, then drain and divide between your serving bowls. Top with a few slices of chicken breast and a handful of the herb salad, then pour over the warm broth to fill up the bowls. Enjoy with the condiments and lime wedges on the side.

VIETNAMESE-STYLE PORK MEATBALLS WITH RICE NOODLES & LEMON GRASS DRESSING

A simple idea where you can riff with whatever crunchy veg and herbs you have in your fridge. The meatballs are inexpensive to make, incredibly quick and easy to pull together and can be prepped in advance. Don't forget to add the pan juices over the meatballs when serving the salad.

Serves 4–6

800g (1lb 12oz) minced pork (15% fat)

2 shallots, finely diced

3 garlic cloves, finely grated or finely chopped

½ red chilli, deseeded and finely chopped

2-cm (¾-inch) piece of fresh root ginger, grated or very finely chopped

1 heaped tablespoon finely chopped fresh coriander stems

1 tablespoon soy sauce

large pinch of flaky sea salt

3 tablespoons olive oil

100ml (3½fl oz) water

50g (1¾oz) roasted salted peanuts, crushed, to serve

For the lemon grass dressing

2 lemon grass stalks

½ red chilli, deseeded and finely chopped

1 teaspoon palm sugar or 1 tablespoon maple syrup

finely grated zest and juice of 2 limes

2 tablespoons soy sauce

2 tablespoons water

1 tablespoon rice vinegar

1 tablespoon fish sauce

1 tablespoon sunflower oil

small pinch of salt

For the noodle salad

100g (3½oz) rice noodles

1 carrot, peeled and finely sliced into matchsticks

½ cucumber, finely sliced into matchsticks

1 banana shallot, finely sliced into matchsticks

small handful of mint, leaves picked

small handful of fresh coriander

small handful of basil

1. To make the meatballs, add the minced pork to a bowl with the shallots, garlic, red chilli, ginger, coriander stems, soy sauce and salt, then scrunch it all up with your hands so that everything is evenly combined. Roll into 16 balls, about 60g (2¼oz) each.

2. Place a large frying pan, big enough to cook all the meatballs without overcrowding and with a lid, over a medium heat and add the olive oil. Add the meatballs and fry for 4–6 minutes, turning every so often so that they are golden on every side.

3. Add the water to the pan, lower the heat and cover with a lid to steam the meatballs for a further 4 minutes until cooked through. Once ready, turn the heat off and let them

rest, covered, while you make the dressing. This will keep them from going dry.

4. Peel away and discard the tough outer layers of the lemon grass stalks, then very finely chop the insides (this is important, as you don't want any large chunks of lemon grass). Mix with all the remaining dressing ingredients in a small bowl.

5. Cook the noodles according to the packet instructions, then drain and rinse under cold running water until completely cooled.

6. To serve, divide the noodles between serving bowls and top with the steamed meatballs and some of the resting juices from the pan. Arrange the veg and herbs on each dish, then spoon over the lemon grass dressing and scatter over the crushed peanuts.

SHREDDED CHICKEN IN 'MALA' SICHUAN DRESSING

When my older sister Amy turned 21 (about 21 years ago), she had a party and enlisted a bunch of girlfriends from her time at the Ballymaloe Cookery School to help cook for all the guests. The starter was from the school's curriculum and called 'Simple Vietnamese Shredded Chicken Salad'. Now, it's only simple when you are shredding for two as in the recipe below, but this party was for more than fifty, so the name was swiftly changed to 'Simple My Arse Shredded Chicken Salad'. The recipe was still on the curriculum when I attended Ballymaloe in 2019. This uses leftover chicken from the whole poached chicken recipe on page 139, but if you want to start from scratch, then simply poach two chicken breasts or thighs as detailed below.

....

Serves 2 as a main, 4 as a starter

200g (7oz) leftover cooked chicken from Chicken Pho Ga (see page 139), shredded, or 2 boneless skinless chicken breasts or thighs

1 quantity Sichuan Peppercorn Dressing (see page 197)

1 Savoy cabbage or 2 Little Gem lettuces, leaves separated

salt

To serve

small bunch of fresh coriander

1 small bunch of radishes (about 5–6), sliced

2 spring onions, finely sliced into rounds

1 small shallot, very finely sliced into rings

1 green chilli, finely sliced into rounds

1 lime, cut into wedges, plus an extra squeeze of juice

½ quantity Fried Peanuts & Crispy Lime Leaves (see page 196, optional)

1. If poaching the chicken instead of using leftovers, then poach them in a pan of salted simmering water for 8–10 minutes, depending on their size, until cooked through. Remove from the water to a plate and allow to cool slightly, then season with salt while warm and shred. Place the shredded chicken in a bowl, add half the dressing and toss together to coat.

2. Blanch the cabbage leaves in salted, boiling water for 2 minutes, then submerge in cold water to stop them from cooking further. If using Gem lettuce, you can skip this step. Place the cabbage or lettuce leaf 'cups' on a large serving platter, then pile on the dressed shredded chicken alongside for people to assemble themselves. Arrange the coriander leaves, radishes, spring onions, shallot, green chilli and lime wedges around.

3. Bring to the table for people to scoop up some of the shredded chicken into a leaf 'cup' with some of the garnishes, more of the dressing and a squeeze of lime juice, topped with some of the fried peanuts and crispy lime leaves, if using.

SESAME CABBAGE WITH POACHED CHICKEN

There is a lot that can be taken from this recipe. Poaching chicken breasts is a process I do regularly, as it's a quick way to get a flavourful broth without the hassle of taking chicken off the bone if you are tight on time – and it's also a great way to keep the breast meat moist. The tahini-dressed cabbage is inspired by the classic Chinese sesame cabbage salad, with the chicken liquor making it extra creamy and full of flavour. It's 10/10 – would recommend!

Serves 2

2 spring onions, roughly chopped

3-cm (1¼-inch) piece of fresh root ginger

1 tablespoon chicken stock powder or 1 chicken stock cube, crumbled

2 boneless skinless chicken breasts

1 sweetheart cabbage (or any white cabbage)

salt

For the sesame dressing

3 tablespoons Chinese sesame paste or tahini

5 tablespoons chicken poaching water (see step 2)

juice of ½ lemon

To serve

1 heaped tablespoon Crispy Chilli Oil (see page 199, or any good-quality shop-bought crispy chilli oil will do), or more/less to taste

jasmine rice or noodles

1. Bring a large pot of water to the boil, then stir in the spring onions, ginger and chicken stock powder or cube, turn down to a low simmer and carefully place your chicken breasts in the water. Poach them for 8–10 minutes, depending on their size, until cooked through.

2. Remove from the water to a plate, reserving 5 tablespoons of the liquor for the dressing, and allow to rest for 5 minutes while you prepare the cabbage.

3. Mix the dressing ingredients together in a large bowl.

4. Finely shred the cabbage into thin ribbons and add this to the dressing in the bowl along with a pinch of salt. Toss it all together so that the cabbage is well coated in the dressing.

5. Pile the cabbage on to a serving plate, then slice the chicken breasts up neatly, place them on top of the cabbage and season with salt. Spoon over as much crispy chilli oil as you want, then serve with a bowl of jasmine rice or noodles.

PORK LAAB WITH RED CURRY MAGIC DUST

This is my take on a Thai laab salad. You could use any minced meat here, but my preference is pork or chicken. Toasted rice is commonly used in Thai cooking to add a nutty flavour and aroma to stir-fries and sauces or as a garnish. My twist is dry-frying the rice with a little Thai red curry paste to give a fiery and fragrant finish. I call it magic dust. When everything is so intense in Thai-style food, thick-cut semi-peeled fresh cucumber makes the perfect palate-cleansing garnish. I love serving this for friends with sticky or coconut rice, with a glass of Gewürztraminer or a Thai beer.

Serves 4

2 tablespoons vegetable or sunflower oil

2 garlic cloves, finely grated

4 lemon grass stalks, finely sliced

6 whole dried red chillies

100ml (3½fl oz) chicken stock or water

500g (1lb 2oz) minced pork (15% fat)

pinch of salt

4 baby shallots, finely sliced into rounds

1 small bunch of spring onions (about 5), thickly sliced into 1-cm (½-inch) pieces

handful of fresh coriander, roughly chopped, plus extra to serve

handful of mint, leaves picked and chopped, plus extra to serve

juice of 1 lime

3 tablespoons fish sauce

For the toasted rice powder

2 tablespoons jasmine rice

2 tablespoons dry Thai red curry paste (I use Mae Ploy)

For the nam pla prik dressing

2–3 bird's-eye chillies, finely sliced (or as much as you want)

1 garlic clove, grated

3 tablespoons fish sauce

finely grated zest and juice of 1 lime

To serve

1 Little Gem lettuce, leaves separated

½ cucumber, peeled in zebra stripes and cut into thick rounds

2 limes, halved

1. Start by making the toasted rice powder. Toast the rice in a dry saucepan over a medium heat for 5–8 minutes, tossing regularly, until it's lightly golden and smells popcorn-y. Now add the curry paste and stir quickly to coat the rice, giving it a good mix off the heat until the paste is evenly distributed. Place back on the heat and continue to toast for 3–4 minutes until the paste has cooked and dried into the rice. Be careful not to burn it, as you want it to stay vibrant and fiery red. Remove from the heat and set aside to cool completely. Once cooled, blitz in a high-speed blender until you have a fine powder.

2. Add the oil to a large frying pan or flameproof casserole, then add the garlic, lemon grass and dried chillies to the cold oil. Place over a medium-low heat and fry for 1 minute until fragrant, then add the chicken stock or water, pork mince and salt and cook, stirring occasionally, over a medium heat for 10 minutes until the pork is cooked through and you barely have any liquid remaining.

3. Turn off the heat and stir in the shallots, spring onions, coriander, mint, lime juice, fish sauce and 4 tablespoons of the toasted rice powder.

4. Mix the dressing ingredients together in a small bowl. (This will keep in a sterilized airtight jar in the fridge for at least a month.)

5. Arrange the lettuce leaves, cucumber, extra coriander, mint and lime halves on one side of a large serving platter. Spoon the minced pork on to the other half and scatter over a generous amount of the toasted rice powder. Serve to the table, allowing people to scoop up the minced pork into lettuce cups and top with a drizzle of the dressing and more of the rice powder if they wish.

THE DINER SALAD

When we were kids, Eddie Rocket's was the coolest place in town. For Jack and I, 'There ain't no finer diner' as is their tagline. It was used by our parents as a bartering tool. Dragged to an interior design shop while Mum pottered for hours, or a weekly Tuesday night Toastmasters event meeting (the only kids in the world that have ever gone to one) with Dad, we were treated to Eddie Rocket's afterwards! Their classic burger is served with a 'secret sauce', which is vibrantly green, briny and sweet, and the inspiration behind the dressing in this salad.

Serves 4–6

6 boneless, skin-on chicken thighs

2 sesame bagels, cut into 1-cm (½-inch) chunks

1 Butterhead lettuce, leaves separated

1 quantity Pickled Celery & Carrots (see page 201)

1 tablespoon chopped dill

salt

hot sauce of your choosing, to serve

For the 'secret sauce' dressing

small handful of dill (15g/½oz), roughly chopped

2 pickled gherkins

1 garlic clove, peeled

1 tablespoon capers

3 tablespoons extra virgin olive oil

1 tablespoon natural yogurt

3 tablespoons mayonnaise

1 teaspoon American mustard (I use French's)

½ tablespoon tomato ketchup

juice of ½ lemon

pinch of flaky sea salt

For the pickled salsa

2 pickled gherkins, diced

½ red onion, finely chopped

1 tablespoon capers

1. Preheat the oven to 220°C (200°C fan, 425°F), Gas Mark 7.

2. Season the chicken thighs with salt, then place, skin-side down, in a nonstick ovenproof frying pan over a medium heat and fry for about 5–8 minutes until the skin is golden and crispy. Then flip over, transfer the pan to the oven and bake for 10–15 minutes until cooked through.

3. While the chicken is in the oven, blitz all the dressing ingredients together in a blender until smooth.

4. Remove the pan from the oven, then transfer the chicken to a plate to rest, leaving you with a layer of chicken juices and fat in the pan. We are going to use this for frying up the chunks of bagel for the croutons – the best flavour secret!

5. Place the pan with the chicken juices and fat over a medium-high heat on the hob. As the pan gets hot, scrape the pan to release all those flavoursome stuck-on bits, then once it starts to sizzle, add the bagel chunks with a pinch of salt and toss them in the juices and fat. Transfer the pan to the oven for 5–8 minutes until lightly golden on each side. Remove from the oven and allow to cool for a few minutes.

6. Mix all the ingredients for the pickled salsa together.

7. Slice the chicken up and add it to a large serving platter with the lettuce, pickled celery and carrots, bagel croutons, dressing, dill and pickled salsa, along with a bottle of hot sauce on the side.

KALE CAESAR

Our take on the classic. I'm sharing the process for roasting a whole chicken, as I think it's a lovely way to serve a Caesar salad, but feel free to adapt the approach to your own situation. There are other elements that make our Caesar salad special – the dressing for sure, but the tomatoes are also key. In the restaurants, we semi-dehydrate them overnight at a very low temperature, which intensifies the flavour to create little sweet bursts of umami. But you can achieve amazing flavour at home in only two hours of cooking, as I show you here.

....

Serves 4

1 whole chicken, about 1.5kg (3lb 5oz)

1 lemon, halved

a few thyme sprigs

olive oil

200g (7oz) streaky bacon

50g (1 ¾oz) curly kale, stalks removed and shredded

Cos lettuce leaves, torn

1 quantity Basil Caesar Dressing (see page 197)

salt

shaved Parmesan cheese, to serve

For the semi-dried tomatoes

250g (9oz) cherry tomatoes

2 garlic cloves, finely grated

1 teaspoon dried oregano

For the garlic croutons

5 slices of sourdough bread, cut into 2-cm (¾-inch) cubes

2–3 tablespoons olive oil

1 tablespoon very finely chopped garlic

1 teaspoon mixed dried herbs, such as rosemary, oregano and thyme

1. Pat the chicken dry with kitchen paper, then season generously with salt both inside and out. Push half a lemon and all the thyme sprigs inside the bird and let it sit for at least 30 minutes to allow the salt to set into the chicken – uncovered overnight in the fridge will give the best result.

2. To make the semi-dried tomatoes, preheat the oven to 150°C (130°C fan, 300°F), Gas Mark 2. Cut the tomatoes in half widthways and sit, cut-sides up, on a baking tray. Season each tomato half with salt, a grating of garlic and a pinch of the dried oregano, then roast for 1½–2 hours or until they have reduced in size, deepened in colour and the flavour has intensified. Remove from the oven and set aside to cool.

3. Take the chicken out of the fridge about an hour before you are ready to roast it to bring it up to room temperature. Set the oven to 210°C (190°C fan, 410°F), Gas Mark 6½.

4. Pat the chicken dry again, then rub olive oil gently all over it. Roast on the middle shelf for about 45 minutes (or as long as recommended for the size of your bird), or until the juices run clear when you pierce the thickest part of the thigh with the tip of a knife. When cooked, remove from the oven and let it rest for 30 minutes.

5. Meanwhile, lay out the bacon slices on a baking tray, then add a sheet of nonstick baking paper on top, followed by another baking tray so that it fits over nicely – this will give you foolproof crisp bacon, as the bacon renders in its own fat. Place on the top shelf in the oven and cook for about 15 minutes until crispy and golden. Remove from the oven and cut into bite-sized pieces.

6. To make the garlic croutons, toss the sourdough cubes with the remaining crouton ingredients and a generous pinch of salt in a bowl. Tip on to a baking tray, spread out in a single layer and roast for 20 minutes, stirring regularly to ensure they toast evenly.

7. Pick the chicken breast and thigh meat off the bone and squeeze the other lemon half over it. (Save the carcass for your stock pot.)

8. Dress the kale and Cos in most of the basil Caesar dressing, then top with shavings of Parmesan and serve everything family-style with the remaining dressing on the side, preferably outside in the sun.

A THAI-STYLE SUMMER STEAK

This recipe relies on top-notch ingredients, so buy the best steak you can afford and use good-quality tomatoes and onions. Although I've given you the process for cooking the onions and steak in a cast iron pan and finishing the onions in the oven, this is best done on a barbecue when you have the chance. For the onions, get them on to the grill early and char them all over, then move to the cooler part of the barbecue to continue to cook until the insides can be almost oozed out of the blackened skin – they are particularly good.

Serves 2

2 sirloin steaks, about 225g (8oz) each

6 calçot onions or large salad onions or baby leeks

2 tablespoons olive oil

1 tablespoon butter (optional)

1 large beef tomato (get the best you can get)

squeeze of lemon juice

flaky sea salt

For the marinade

2 tablespoons Golden Mountain Seasoning Sauce or oyster sauce

1 tablespoon soy sauce

1 tablespoon fish sauce

For the nam pla prik dressing

4 Pickled Bird's-eye Chillies (see page 201), finely chopped

4 garlic cloves, finely chopped

3 tablespoons fish sauce

juice of 2–3 limes (about 4 tablespoons), plus extra if needed

1. Start by marinating the steak. Take the steak out of the fridge 30 minutes beforehand. Mix the marinade ingredients together in a shallow dish, add the steak and turn until well coated. Set aside at room temperature for at least 10 minutes.

2. Preheat the oven to 210°C (190°C fan, 410°F), Gas Mark 6½.

3. Place a cast iron pan over a high heat. Keep the onions or baby leeks whole and drizzle them with 1 tablespoon of the olive oil and season with a pinch of salt. Once the pan is smoking hot, add the onions and cook for about 8–10 minutes until heavily charred on all sides. Transfer the onions to a low-sided roasting tray and roast in the oven for 20 minutes until very soft.

4. Keeping the pan smoking hot, remove the steak from the marinade and rub with the remaining 1 tablespoon of oil until coated all over, then season with salt. Add the steak to the pan and cook for 1–2 minutes on each side for medium-rare (the cooking time will differ depending on the thickness and size of your steak). If you've got a nice sirloin steak that has fat running down the side, flip it on to the fat side and fry for 1 minute until the fat has rendered and is golden. Remove from the pan to a plate and allow to rest for at least 10 minutes. After this, you can add the steak back to the pan over a low heat and add the butter, if using, and baste the steak in it for 30 seconds on each side.

5. To make the dressing, add the pickled chillies and garlic to a small bowl with the fish sauce and lime juice. Taste for seasoning and add a little more lime juice if necessary.

6. Slice the steak, reserving the resting juices.

7. Slice the tomato, lay on a serving plate or platter and season with salt. Drape over the soft charred onions and the slices of steak with the resting juices, then drizzle with the dressing and add a squeeze of lemon juice.

BEEF & CELERIAC REMOULADE

Celeriac has such versatility. It can be treated like a piece of meat, as in the recipe for Slow-roasted Celeriac on page 65, or thinly sliced and used in a slaw for remoulade as here. Again, buy the best-quality beef steaks you can here for the optimum result.

Serves 2 hungry people or 4

2 fillet steaks, about 225g (8oz) each

2 tablespoons olive oil

1 tablespoon butter

10 sage leaves

flaky sea salt and freshly ground black pepper

English mustard, to serve (optional)

For the horseradish remoulade

½ celeriac

juice of 1 lemon

2-cm (¾-inch) piece of fresh horseradish, peeled and grated, plus extra for garnish, or 1 small teaspoon creamed horseradish

2 tablespoons mayonnaise

1 tablespoon wholegrain mustard

100g (3½oz) frozen edamame beans, defrosted

1. Take the steaks out of the fridge at least 30 minutes before cooking. Season with a big pinch of salt and rub with the olive oil until coated all over.

2. Place a cast iron pan over a high heat. Once smoking hot, add the steaks and cook for 2–3 minutes on each side for medium-rare (the cooking time will differ depending on the thickness and size of the steaks). Reduce the heat to low, add the butter to the pan and baste the steaks in it. Remove the steaks from the pan to a plate and allow to rest for 10 minutes.

3. While the butter is still hot, add the sage leaves to the pan and stir for 10–20 seconds until they crisp up, then remove from the pan and set aside.

4. Meanwhile, make the remoulade. Peel the celeriac, then slice into thin strips the size of matchsticks and add to a bowl. Immediately squeeze over the lemon juice to stop it from discolouring but also to tenderize it. Add the horseradish, mayonnaise and wholegrain mustard, season to taste with salt and pepper and stir to coat. Finally, add the edamame beans and very lightly toss to combine. Taste and adjust the seasoning.

5. Cut the steaks in half, and place on serving plates with a pile of remoulade, the crispy sage leaves, a grating of fresh horseradish and a few twists of black pepper to finish. Serve with English mustard on the side accompanied by a glass of wine, if you like.

A BLT SALAD WITH A STACK OF BUTTERED TOAST

This is a classic sandwich for a reason, but not all BLTs are created equally. Sure, it comes down to the ingredients, but also how you treat them. There is a café called Foodgame in Beggars Bush, Dublin that puts a sweet roasted tomato and spicy mayo in theirs. It's delicious and I would say the best BLT in town. The blistered tomatoes in this recipe could improve most things, and for me the mother of all dressing, the Caesar, is not just for its namesake salad. This makes a lovely breakfast, brunch or lunch salad for a casual family or friends' get-together.

....

Serves 4

250g (9oz) cherry tomatoes

2 tablespoons olive oil

1 tablespoon runny honey

1 teaspoon flaky sea salt

250g (9oz) streaky bacon

1 Butterhead, Little Gem or Cos lettuce, or any lettuce of your choice

1 quantity Basil Caesar Dressing (see page 197)

4–8 slices of bread, toasted and buttered, to serve

1. Preheat the oven to 240°C (220°C fan, 475°F), Gas Mark 9.

2. Put the tomatoes in a small roasting tray with the olive oil, honey and salt. You want the tomatoes to all fit snugly so that they roast evenly together. Roast on the middle shelf for 15–20 minutes until the tomatoes are a little charred on top and soft.

3. While the tomatoes are roasting, lay out all the bacon slices on a baking tray, then add a sheet of nonstick baking paper on top of the bacon, followed by another baking tray so that it fits over nicely. This will give you evenly crisp bacon and is foolproof, as the bacon renders in its own fat. Place in the oven on the top shelf and cook for about 15 minutes until crispy and golden.

4. Remove the bacon and tomatoes from the oven.

5. Add the lettuce to a large serving platter or salad bowl. Roughly chop the bacon into large chunks and add to the lettuce with the tomatoes. Drizzle over the basil Casaer dressing and serve immediately with a stack of the buttered toast.

THAI RED CURRY SPATCHCOCKED CHICKEN WITH A MOUNTAIN OF HERB SALAD

This dish, like most of my recipe ideas, is best eaten with a spoon. You are basically making a Thai red curry-style base, then sitting a whole flattened chicken on top to roast. The chicken juices run into the sauce, creating the most outrageously delicious curry. The mayonnaise marinade might throw you, but it's key to keeping the chicken moist while cooking on such a high heat. The curry is rich, but with the fish sauce, lime juice and herb salad it becomes quite tangy, fresh and light. Feel free to adapt the recipe by using chicken legs or bone-in thighs for an easier preparation.

Serves 4

3 tablespoons mayonnaise

2 tablespoons olive oil

1 teaspoon chilli powder

1 whole chicken, about 1.5kg (3lb 5oz), spatchcocked (ask your butcher do this for you or look up a YouTube video and do it yourself, it's very easy!)

3 tablespoons vegetable or sunflower oil

3-cm (1¼-inch) piece of fresh root ginger, peeled and finely grated

3 garlic cloves, finely grated

2 heaped tablespoons dry Thai red curry paste (I use Mae Ploy)

400ml (14fl oz) can full-fat coconut milk

400g (14oz) cherry tomatoes

1 tablespoon fish sauce

juice of 1 lime

salt

jasmine rice, sticky rice or noodles, to serve (optional)

For the herb salad

30g (1oz) basil leaves

30g (1oz) mint, leaves picked

30g (1oz) fresh coriander leaves

1 bunch of spring onions (about 5), finely sliced into long thin strips

juice of 1 lime, plus extra to serve

1. Mix the mayonnaise, olive oil and chilli powder in a small bowl.

2. Pat the spatchcocked chicken dry all over with kitchen paper. Press the chicken down on the breast so that the breastbone cracks a little so your chicken will lay flat. Season the chicken with 1 teaspoon of salt, rubbing it into every bit of the chicken skin. Now pour the mayonnaise mixture all over the chicken and again rub it all over so that every bit is coated. Cover and allow to marinate at room temperature for 30 minutes. If you are preparing the chicken ahead of time, place the chicken in the fridge to marinate overnight.

3. When you're ready to cook, preheat the oven to its hottest setting.

4. Heat the vegetable or sunflower oil in an ovenproof pan, wide enough to snugly accommodate the chicken, over a medium-high heat. Add the ginger, garlic and red curry paste to the oil and fry for 3–5 minutes until it has absorbed the oil and is smelling fragrant – it's important to caramelize the paste slightly.

5. Stir in the coconut milk, then half-fill the empty can with water and add along with the tomatoes. Bring to a simmer, then carefully place the chicken on top of the sauce, spreading the legs out to expose as much of the skin as possible to the direct heat of the oven.

6. Transfer the pan to the oven and roast the chicken for 45 minutes, or until the juices run clear when you pierce the thickest part of the bird with the tip of a knife and the skin is dark golden and crispy.

7. Remove the pan from the oven and carefully transfer the chicken to a plate to rest for 20–30 minutes. Then stir the fish sauce and lime juice into the sauce in the pan and taste for seasoning.

8. For the herb salad, toss the herbs and spring onions with the lime juice and a pinch of salt in a bowl.

9. Carve up the chicken into 2 breasts, 2 thighs and 2 drumsticks. Spoon a few ladles of the sauce into a serving bowl, then place the chicken on top. Serve with the herb salad and extra lime juice. Heat the rest of the sauce up in a small saucepan, then serve to the table with a big pot of jasmine rice, sticky rice or noodles, or just as is.

SPICY LAMB MEATBALLS WITH GARLIC YOGURT & SALSA VERDE

The combination of lamb, yogurt and salsa verde always gets me going. You could easily cheat here and buy lamb koftas from the butcher or supermarket, and use what salad or vegetable leaves you have to hand to serve.

....

Serves 2–4

500g (1lb 2oz) minced lamb

50g (1¾oz) breadcrumbs soaked in 50g (1¾oz) natural yogurt

3 garlic cloves, finely grated

handful of mint, leaves picked and finely chopped

2 teaspoons ground cumin

1 teaspoon ground coriander

1 teaspoon chilli powder

3 tablespoons vegetable oil

50ml (2fl oz) water

salt and freshly ground black pepper

For the garlic yogurt

4 tablespoons natural yogurt

2 tablespoons extra virgin olive oil

1 garlic clove, finely grated

For the salsa verde

small handful of fresh coriander (about 10g/¼oz)

small handful of flat leaf parsley (about 10g/¼oz)

small handful of mint (about 10g/¼oz), leaves picked

6 green or Kalamata olives, pitted

½ green chilli, deseeded

3 tablespoons extra virgin olive oil

juice of ½ lemon

For the pickled onion

1 red onion, halved and finely sliced into half-moons

juice of ½ lemon

To serve

100g (3½oz) salad leaves

seeds of 1 pomegranate

½ teaspoon sumac or sweet paprika

1. For the meatballs, mix together the minced lamb, soaked breadcrumbs, garlic, mint and spices in a bowl with a pinch of salt and a few generous grinds of black pepper until evenly combined. Roll the mixture into large golf ball-sized meatballs, then set aside on a plate.

2. Mix the garlic yogurt ingredients together in a small bowl and set aside.

3. For the salsa verde, finely chop the herbs, olives and green chilli together on a chopping board, then scoop into a bowl. Add the extra virgin olive oil along with a pinch of salt and the lemon juice.

4. Heat the vegetable oil in a large frying pan with a lid over a medium-high heat. Once hot, add the meatballs and fry for 5 minutes until evenly golden on all sides. Turn the heat down, then add the measured water, cover the pan with the lid and steam for about 5 minutes until cooked through.

5. Turn off the heat and allow the meatballs to rest for 5 minutes.

6. For the pickled onion, place the red onion in a small bowl, squeeze over the lemon juice and add a pinch of salt. Scrunch the onion together with your hands so that it's coated in the lemon juice and starts to turn bright pink.

7. Serve everything to the table for people to assemble their own bowls, starting with the salad leaves, followed by the meatballs with a few spoonfuls of the juice at the bottom of the pan, then drizzling over the garlic yogurt and salsa verde, topping with the pickled onion and finally sprinkling over the pomegranate seeds and the sumac or sweet paprika.

ROAST CHICKEN WINTER PANZANELLA

This is a one-tin 'wonder' salad! Roasting a chicken over vegetables is one of the most comforting, wholesome cooking techniques, its juices raining over the squash to create the most delicious seasoning. You can make this without the roasted garlic dressing and just finish with extra virgin olive oil and lemon juice, but you might as well, given that you are roasting the chicken and squash anyway, and roasting a whole bulb of garlic is never a bad idea.

Serves 4

1 whole chicken, about 1.5kg (3lb 5oz)

1 butternut squash, about 1kg (2lb 4oz)

2 garlic bulbs

small handful of thyme, plus a few extra sprigs

2 tablespoons olive oil

½ lemon

2 slices of sourdough bread

200g (7oz) cavolo nero

salt and freshly ground black pepper

For the roasted garlic dressing

4 tablespoons extra virgin olive oil

juice of ½ lemon

1 tablespoon sherry vinegar

1 tablespoon runny honey

1 teaspoon Dijon mustard

½ teaspoon white miso paste

1 egg yolk

For the parsley & caper salad

1 tablespoon capers

1 onion, finely sliced

large handful of flat leaf parsley (15g/½oz)

1. Take the chicken out of the fridge about an hour before cooking it to bring it up to room temperature, which will result in a more evenly cooked and moist roast chicken.

2. Preheat the oven to 210°C (190°C fan, 410°F), Gas Mark 6½.

3. Cut the butternut squash in half lengthways and scoop out the seeds, then cut into half-moon slices about 2cm (¾ inch) thick. Place them in a large roasting tray with the garlic bulbs, the small handful of thyme, the olive oil and salt and pepper. Toss it all together with your hands so that everything is coated in the oil and seasoning.

4. Place the chicken on a grill rack over the roasting tray to act as a trivet and raise the chicken above the vegetables so that the fat will drip into the roasting tray. Season with salt and pepper, then place the lemon half inside the chicken cavity with the extra thyme sprigs and roast for 40–50 minutes, or until the juices run clear when you pierce the thickest part of the thigh with the tip of a knife and the skin is golden and crispy.

5. Remove from the oven, lift off the rack and transfer the chicken and roast garlic to a plate. Turn the squash over. Tear the bread into 2-cm (¾-inch) chunks, then add to the tray with the squash and chicken juices and roast for 10 minutes to crisp up.

6. Meanwhile, remove the stalks from the cavolo nero and tear the leaves into small pieces, then wash, leaving the leaves a little wet. Remove the roasting tray from the oven and add the cavolo nero on top. Take the lemon half out of the chicken cavity and squeeze it over the kale, then place the tray back in the oven for 5 minutes.

7. To make the dressing, squeeze out the roasted garlic from the skins of the cloves into a small bowl, add all the other dressing ingredients, season with salt and pepper and blitz with a hand blender (or use whatever blender you have) until smooth and creamy.

8. Mix the parsley and caper salad ingredients together in a bowl.

9. Carve up the chicken and serve alongside the kale, squash and crunchy bread, the dressing and the salad.

MIDDLE EASTERN CHICKEN PLATE

This is always one of our top sellers in the restaurants. The key to the delicious harissa-marinated chicken thighs is to cook them in a hot oven so that the skin gets super crispy. Don't feel you have to make all the elements from scratch here – it's very easy to shortcut by buying flatbreads, hummus, pickles and olives or simply using yogurt and tahini as the sauces. If you do make all the components, serve them on large plates and allow everyone to help themselves (pictured overleaf).

Serves 4–6 (depending on who you're feeding!)

8 chicken thighs

1 quantity Hummus (see opposite)

1 quantity Zhoug (see opposite)

1 quantity Pickled Red Cabbage (see page 201)

1 quantity Aubergine & Preserved Lemon (see page 97)

1 quantity Maple Spiced Pumpkin Seeds (see page 196)

1 quantity Yogurt Flatbreads (see opposite)

salt and freshly ground black pepper

For the harissa marinade

1 tablespoon cumin seeds

1 tablespoon coriander seeds

2 tablespoons harissa

2 tablespoons olive oil

3 garlic cloves, finely grated

1. Preheat the oven to 220°C (200°C fan, 425°F), Gas Mark 7.

2. To make the harissa marinade, crush the cumin and coriander seeds using a pestle and mortar, then mix with the remaining marinade ingredients along with a big pinch of salt and a generous grind of black pepper.

3. Put the chicken thighs in a low-sided roasting tray with the harissa marinade and give it all a good mix with your hands so that the chicken is nicely coated. Season the chicken with another pinch of salt on top of each thigh, then roast for 45 minutes until the skin is crispy, golden and a little blackened on the top.

4. Remove the chicken from the oven and allow it to rest for a few minutes.

5. Serve everything at the table family-style, allowing each person to build their own plate.

HUMMUS

There are a few key steps to ensuring a creamy, silky-smooth hummus: cook your chickpeas until they're nice and soft, blend them while warm and for a long time and finally add a cube of ice towards the end to get a nice glossy finish (pictured opposite).

....

540g (1lb 3oz) jar chickpeas (400g/14oz drained weight)

1 garlic clove, peeled

1 tablespoon tahini

juice of ½ lemon

1 tablespoon extra virgin olive oil, plus extra to garnish

pinch of flaky sea salt

1 ice cube

sliced pickled guindilla peppers, to garnish (optional)

1. Put the chickpeas with all their liquid in a small saucepan and bring to a low simmer for 5 minutes. Transfer the chickpeas and half the liquid to a high-speed blender, add all the remaining ingredients, except the ice cube, and blitz for 1 minute until smooth, adding a little more chickpea liquid if you want your hummus smoother or less thick. Now add the ice cube and blitz again for a minute until very smooth and silky.

2. Serve drizzled with olive oil and with a scattering of pickled guindilla peppers if you like.

ZHOUG

Zhoug, zhug or shkug, whichever form its name takes this classic Middle Eastern green sauce is made with olive oil, herbs and green chilli. When I was in Israel it was served with nearly every meal. It's rich, herby and spicy and I love it. My twist is adding some pickled green chilli to give it a little acidity, which lightens it. I also always add a spoonful of the pickling liquor to taste once it's blended.

....

2–3 pickled guindilla hot peppers or 2 tablespoons pickled sliced jalapeños, plus 1 tablespoon brine from the jar

2 green chillies

1 garlic clove, peeled

handful of flat leaf parsley, stems and all (about 15g/½oz)

handful of fresh coriander, stems and all (about 15g/½oz)

75ml (2½fl oz) extra virgin olive oil

1 teaspoon cumin seeds

½ teaspoon salt

generous amount of freshly ground black pepper (about 6 grinds)

1. Blitz all the ingredients together in a blender until you have a smooth green sauce.

YOGURT FLATBREADS

I appreciate the time and effort that craftspeople like bakers put into creating their amazing products, and I'm a big lover of sourdough, but I like to cook some breads instinctively, without scales and usually with recipes that come together immediately. These flatbreads do that for me. Using equal parts yogurt to flour, there is no proper kneading required and you have fresh bread in minutes.

....

350g (12oz) natural yogurt

350g (12oz) self-raising flour, plus extra for dusting

1 teaspoon baking powder

large pinch of salt

1. Mix all the ingredients together in a large bowl until they form a rough dough. Turn out on to a floured surface and knead for a minute until you have a smooth-ish dough. You don't need to knead this dough properly, as it's not yeasted.

2. Place a heavy-based pan such as a griddle pan or frying pan over a high heat.

3. Cut the dough into 4–6 equal pieces, then shape each into a ball. Flour the surface again and a rolling pin, then roll out each ball into a round about 1cm (½ inch) thick. You might have to re-flour the surface as you go so that they don't stick.

4. Add a flatbread to the hot pan and cook for 1 minute on each side until golden and puffed up a little. Remove from the pan and repeat with the remaining flatbreads.

THINGS FROM THE SEA

THAI-STYLE CASHEW NOODLES WITH CHARRED ZINGY PRAWNS

The dressing is the star here and adding the dry Thai red curry paste is my little quick trick to making this an incredible salad. The curry paste you want here is the kind that comes in a pot containing a bag of the paste – I use Mae Ploy. If you can't find cashew butter, it's easy to make: blitz 150g (5½oz) of raw cashew nuts in a high-speed blender until they form a paste. Now add a tablespoon of cold water and blend again until you have a smooth mixture. To this you can now add the remaining dressing ingredients and blend all together. You can also use peanut butter instead. I tend to have a huge bag of frozen raw prawns in the freezer – you can buy really good-quality frozen prawns in an Asian supermarket or from your fishmonger.

Serves 4

24 frozen raw peeled king prawns (6 per person), defrosted

1 tablespoon olive oil

juice of 1 lime, plus 1 lime cut into wedges to serve

1 tablespoon chilli oil of your choice (you can add more or less here, or none at all)

2 nests of egg noodles

1 red pepper, cored, deseeded and thinly sliced into matchsticks

½ cucumber, thinly sliced into matchsticks

small handful of Thai basil or regular basil, leaves picked

small handful of mint, leaves picked

small handful of fresh coriander sprigs

1 banana shallot, finely sliced into matchsticks

2 chillies, finely sliced

2 spring onions, finely sliced diagonally

salt

For the cashew butter dressing

150g (5½oz) cashew butter (see recipe introduction)

3-cm (1¼-inch) piece of fresh root ginger, peeled

juice of 1 lime, plus extra if needed

3 tablespoons sunflower oil

3 tablespoons rice vinegar

2 tablespoons soy sauce

2 tablespoons fish sauce

1 tablespoon maple syrup

1 tablespoon water

2 garlic cloves, peeled

2 teaspoons dry Thai red curry paste (see recipe introduction)

1. To make the cashew dressing, blitz all the ingredients in a high-speed blender until thick and creamy. Taste for seasoning – if your lime wasn't very juicy, you may have to add a little more lime juice.

2. Once the prawns have defrosted, pat them completely dry with kitchen paper, then drizzle with the olive oil and sprinkle all over with salt.

3. Heat a griddle pan over a high heat, and once hot, add the prawns and cook for 30 seconds on each side or until pink and cooked through. Transfer to a plate and squeeze over the lime juice and add the chilli oil, if using.

4. Cook the noodles according to the packet instructions, then drain and rinse under cold running water until completely cooled. Drain well, then add to a bowl with about three-quarters of the dressing (you can add as much or as little as you want here, but I like my noodles well sauced).

5. Pile the noodles on to a serving plate or into individual bowls, then serve with the grilled prawns, red pepper, cucumber, the herbs, shallot, chillies, spring onion, and with more dressing on top and lime wedges on the side.

FISH FINGER 'SALAD'

This is for my 'godmother'– her title is in inverted commas because she was bestowed this role when, aged 12, I asked her if she'd be mine. I was never baptized, but she accepted, poured water on my head, and it turned out to be the best decision I ever made, as she has guided me throughout my life – if she hadn't said the words, 'you light up when you talk about food' I may never have got here. Enough mush, my godmother always celebrates a win with a cold glass of fizz and a fish finger sandwich, which I love about her! At New Year's Eve, to much delight, I made elevated fish finger sandwiches in her honour, and thought why not turn them into a salad? For ease, shop-bought frozen fish fingers are welcomed and encouraged.

....

Serves 4

50g (1¾oz) plain flour

2 eggs

70g (2½oz) breadcrumbs

1 spring onion, finely chopped

½ red chilli, deseeded and finely chopped

good pinch of flaky sea salt and freshly ground black pepper

4 skinless fillets of any chunky white fish (I like cod, haddock or hake), about 150g (5½oz) each

4 tablespoons olive oil, plus extra if needed

2 Little Gem lettuces, shredded

lemon wedges, to serve

1 quantity Salsa Verde (see page 46)

For the garlic mayonnaise

3 tablespoons mayonnaise

½ garlic clove, grated

juice of ½ lemon

a few chives, finely chopped

1. Set up your breading station for the fish: lay out 3 bowls in front of you – put the flour in the first bowl, beat the eggs together in the second bowl and mix together the breadcrumbs, spring onion, red chilli and salt and pepper in the third bowl.

2. Keeping one hand for the dry ingredients and one hand for the wet ingredients, dip the first fish fillet in the flour, making sure it's completely coated, then dip it in the beaten egg (using the other hand), again making sure it's completely coated, then finally in the breadcrumb mixture (switching to the first hand), moving the fish around in it so that every bit is covered. Place on a plate on the side and repeat with the remaining 3 fillets.

3. Line a plate with kitchen paper. Heat the olive oil in a frying pan over a medium-high heat. Once hot, add 2 breaded fish fillets to the pan at a time, to avoid overcrowding, and cook for about 3 minutes on each side until golden, crispy and cooked in the middle. Remove from the pan on to the paper-lined plate, then add a little more oil if needed and repeat with the remaining 2 breaded fish.

4. While the fish is cooking, mix the garlic mayonnaise ingredients together in a small bowl, seasoning to taste with salt.

5. To serve, lay out the shredded lettuce on a serving plate, then top with the breaded fish and squeeze over some lemon juice. Dress with the garlic mayo and salsa verde.

CRISPY THAI-STYLE FISH SALAD

Again, shop-bought frozen fish fingers could be used for convenience here, which I always keep in my freezer. In this recipe, the breadcrumbs are textured with spring onion and chilli, adding both visual and flavour interest. Finely shredded Gem lettuce is the perfect bed for the crispy fish and spicy dressing.

....

Serves 4

50g (1¾oz) plain flour

2 eggs

70g (2½oz) breadcrumbs

1 spring onion, finely chopped

½ red chilli, deseeded and finely chopped

good pinch of flaky sea salt and freshly ground black pepper

4 skinless fillets of any chunky white fish (I like cod, haddock or hake), about 150g (5½oz) each (or use 4 frozen fish fingers and cook according to the packet instructions)

4 tablespoons olive oil, plus extra if needed

For the chilli & lime dressing

2–3 bird's-eye chillies, finely sliced (use as little or as much as you want)

1 garlic clove, grated

3 tablespoons fish sauce

finely grated zest and juice of 1 lime

To serve

2 Little Gem lettuces, finely shredded

2 spring onions, finely sliced

small handful of fresh coriander, leaves picked

small handful of Thai basil or regular basil leaves

juice of 1 lime

1. Set up your breading station for the fish. Lay out 3 bowls in front of you. Put the flour in the first bowl, beat the eggs together in the second bowl and mix together the breadcrumbs, spring onion, red chilli and salt and pepper in the third bowl.

2. Keeping one hand for the dry ingredients and one hand for the wet ingredients, dip the first fish fillet in the flour, making sure it's completely coated, then dip it in the beaten egg (using the other hand), again making sure it's completely coated, then finally in the breadcrumb mixture (switching to the first hand), moving the fish around in it so that every bit is covered. Place on a plate on the side and repeat with the remaining 3 fillets.

3. Line a plate with kitchen paper. Heat the olive oil in a frying pan over a medium-high heat. Once hot, add 2 breaded fish fillets to avoid overcrowding the pan and cook for about 3 minutes on each side until golden, crispy and cooked in the middle. Remove from the pan on to the paper-lined plate, then add a little more oil if needed and repeat with the remaining 2 breaded fish fillets.

4. While the fish is cooking, mix the dressing ingredients together in a small bowl.

5. To serve, lay the finely shredded Gem lettuce on a serving plate, scatter the finely sliced spring onions and fresh herbs over, then place the crispy fish fillets on top. Finally, pour the dressing generously over the dish. This can be served either in individual portions or as a large sharing platter.

MISO TROUT & PICKLED NOODLE SALAD

Another purpose for our master miso maple recipe, this time for marinating our trout. Under the hot grill it caramelizes on the fish for a really delicious result. The trout is rich but sits on a sharp and tangy fresh rice noodle salad. This is a healthy, light dish yet without seeming like you're making any sacrifices.

......

Serves 2

300g (10½oz) trout fillet (or salmon fillet)

1 quantity Miso Maple Marinade (see page 199)

150g (5½oz) rice noodles, or any noodles of your choice

2 small handfuls of Pickled Daikon & Carrots (see page 201)

finely grated zest and juice of 1 lime

50g (1¾oz) roasted salted peanuts

a handful of fresh coriander, leaves picked

flaky sea salt

1. Preheat the grill to its highest setting. Line a roasting tray with a large piece of nonstick baking paper or foil, then place the fish in the middle. Pour 3 tablespoons of the miso maple marinade over the fish and allow to sit for 10 minutes.

2. While the fish is marinating, cook the noodles according to the packet instructions, then drain and rinse under cold running water until completely cooled. Drain well, add to a bowl with the lime juice and a tablespoon of the pickling liquor and toss to coat. If the noodles are extra-long ones, feel free to snip them in half so that they are easier to dress (and eat!).

3. Grill the fish, still on its paper or foil, for 6–8 minutes until just cooked and soft in the middle (the cooking time may differ depending on the size of fillet you have, but I err on the side of less).

4. While the fish is cooking, crush the peanuts, then toss with the lime zest to coat.

5. Remove the roasting tray from the oven and slide the lining paper or foil with the fish on to a board to let it rest and to stop it cooking any further. The marinade will have caramelized on top with some charred bits. Brush with any remaining marinade to glaze it further.

6. Divide the noodles between 2 bowls, then top with a chunk of fish and an extra spoonful of the marinade. Serve the pickled daikon and carrots alongside. Finish with a scattering of the crushed peanuts and the coriander, and a little flaky sea salt over the fish.

BUTTERFLIED MACKEREL WITH LABNEH TWO WAYS

Labneh is a super-creamy and luxurious strained yogurt and I love its contrast with spicy food. You can add flavour in many ways, with a little garlic or blanched and blended wild garlic if you can find some. This is a simple preparation, but served with a fresh herby zhoug sauce. Two recipes follow here, one winter and another summer, paired with beautifully butterflied mackerel.

Serves 2–4

2 tablespoons capers

2 butterflied mackerel
or 4 mackerel fillets

2 tablespoons olive oil

squeeze of lemon juice

flaky sea salt and freshly ground
black pepper

1 quantity Zhoug (see page 165),
to serve

For the labneh

500g (1lb 2oz) tub Greek yogurt or
full-fat natural yogurt

½ teaspoon salt

For winter (pictured opposite)

85g (3oz) raw skin-on hazelnuts
(or use ready-roasted, skinned)

2 tablespoons olive oil

4 whole ready-cooked fresh
beetroot (not in vinegar),
quartered

a few sprigs of dill, to garnish

For summer (pictured overleaf)

2 tablespoons olive oil

4 large plum tomatoes or 250g
(9oz) cherry tomatoes, halved

3 spring onions, trimmed then cut
lengthways into 3

1. Start by making the labneh the day before you want to use it. Mix the yogurt and salt together. Line a deep bowl with muslin or cheesecloth or a tea towel. Tip the yogurt into the bowl, then bring the corners of the cloth together into a bundle and tie a knot around the yogurt. Hang over a bowl or tie around the kitchen tap over a bowl so that the liquid drips into the bowl and leave overnight. Alternatively, set a sieve over a bowl and line with the muslin or cheesecloth, then leave to drain overnight.

For winter: If roasting the hazelnuts yourself, preheat the oven to 200°C (180°C fan, 400°F), Gas Mark 6. Spread the hazelnuts out on a baking tray and roast for about 8–10 minutes until golden brown. Remove from the oven and allow to cool for 5 minutes, then tip the nuts on to a clean tea towel and rub them to remove the skins. Roughly chop the nuts and set aside. Place a large frying pan over a high heat and add the olive oil, followed by the beetroot pieces. Fry for 2–3 minutes on each side until a little charred and crisp.

For summer: Place a large frying pan over a high heat and add the olive oil, followed by the tomatoes and spring onions. Fry for 2–3 minutes on all sides until the tomatoes are charred and softened.

2. Transfer the beetroot or tomatoes and spring onions to a bowl with the capers.

3. When ready to cook the fish, pat the mackerel dry on both sides with kitchen paper, then season with flaky sea salt.

4. Heat a frying pan, add the olive oil, then add the mackerel, skin-side down, pressing the skin on to the hot pan so that all the skin is in contact with the hot oil at the same time. Leave to cook for 2–3 minutes until the skin crisps up (if you turn it over too soon, the skin will stick to the pan). I like to cook the fish 90% skin-side down and then only flip it over for a final 10 seconds to finish it off. This way you get a perfectly cooked and light flaky fish, and a crispy skin. Remove the mackerel from the pan to a plate and allow to rest for a minute.

5. Spread the labneh out on a serving platter, then spoon over the beetroot or tomatoes and spring onions and the capers with any juices they may have. Carefully place the mackerel on top, then finish with the zhoug, a squeeze of lemon juice, the hazelnuts, for winter, and a little extra salt and pepper if needed.

A PRAWN COCKTAIL SALAD

I love a good old-fashioned restaurant that does the classics well: oysters, prawn cocktails and a rare burger – that's comfort for me, and my brother too. A quality prawn cocktail relies on fresh ingredients served nice and cold. Crunchy Little Gem lettuce, tangy cocktail sauce and juicy prawns; you can't beat it! I've added a few simple refinements here to elevate the classic still further, such as the dusting of paprika salt and the avocado and hazelnut salsa, which also makes a great topping for soups to add texture. I like to buy skin-on hazelnuts, then roast and skin them myself, as I think you get a much better flavour than the ready-roasted or blanched ones. But if you can't get hold of them or don't have the time to prepare them, don't worry!

Serves 4

250g (9oz) fresh peeled raw prawns, tails left on

1 Little Gem lettuce, leaves separated

1 teaspoon Paprika Salt (see page 71)

salt and freshly ground black pepper

1 small red onion, halved and finely sliced into half-moons

1 heaped tablespoon chopped chives, to garnish

1 lemon, cut into slices, to serve

For the cocktail sauce

3 tablespoons mayonnaise

2 tablespoons tomato ketchup

1 tablespoon extra virgin olive oil

1 heaped teaspoon Dijon mustard

½ garlic clove, finely grated

½ teaspoon sweet paprika

juice of 1 lemon

For the avocado & hazelnut salsa

100g (3½oz) raw skin-on hazelnuts (or use ready-roasted, skinned ones)

1 avocado

1. If roasting the hazelnuts yourself for the avocado and hazelnut salsa, preheat the oven to 200°C (180°C fan, 400°F), Gas Mark 6.

2. Spread the hazelnuts out on a baking tray and roast for about 8–10 minutes until golden brown. Remove from the oven and allow to cool for 5 minutes, then add the nuts to a clean tea towel and rub them inside the tea towel to remove the skins. Roughly chop the nuts and set aside in a bowl.

3. Bring a saucepan of water to the boil and add 1 teaspoon of salt. Once boiling, add the prawns and cook for 2–3 minutes, or until they turn pink. Drain, then add to a bowl of iced water to chill.

4. Mix all the cocktail sauce ingredients together in a small bowl, seasoning with salt and pepper, and stir until you have a smooth, light pink sauce.

5. To finish the avocado and hazelnut salsa, halve, stone and peel the avocado, then cut into 1-cm (½-inch) cubes. Add to the bowl of chopped and roasted hazelnuts and lightly toss together.

6. To assemble, arrange the lettuce around the edge of a serving platter, then add the red onion, avocado and hazelnut salsa on top. Place the cocktail sauce in the middle of the lettuce, and arrange the drained chilled prawns around the edge of the bowl. Serve scattered with chopped chives and a dusting of the paprika salt, with the lemon slices on the side. Alternatively, assemble individual plates with all the salad components and top with the prawns, dressing, paprika salt and a big wedge of lemon.

ZINGY TUNA SASHIMI WITH APPLE & CRISPY THINGS

Turn on the fryer babes, we are making tuna salad. If there is a tuna tostada on a menu, I am ordering. This is a great starter to kick off an evening – the dressing is intensely zingy, the apple brings sweetness and all the salty crispy bits bring very good times. Make sure to buy the freshest sushi-grade tuna you can, as it's crucial for this dish to work.

....

Serves 2 as a main, 4 as a starter

1 quantity Crispy Shallots, using 6 baby or 2 large banana shallots, oil reserved (see page 196)

4 tortillas, cut into quarters or triangles

300g (10½oz) sushi-grade tuna

1 small sweet red apple

2 tablespoons roasted salted peanuts

1 green chilli, sliced

small handful of fresh coriander, leaves picked

salt

For the ginger dressing

2-cm (¾-inch) piece of fresh root ginger, peeled and very finely chopped or finely grated

1 garlic clove, finely grated

2 tablespoons rice vinegar

2 tablespoons soy sauce

juice of 1 lime

½ tablespoon maple syrup

2 tablespoons sunflower oil

1. To make the crispy tortillas, carefully pour the reserved crispy shallot oil into a saucepan pan, place it over a medium-high heat and heat up. Test that the oil is hot enough by tearing off a little piece of tortilla and adding it to the hot oil – if it bubbles up and floats, you're ready to go.

2. Add the tortilla quarters or triangles to the hot oil (you might have to do this in batches) and fry for about 2 minutes until lightly golden and crisp. Lift out with a slotted spoon into the sieve set over the bowl you used for the crispy shallots, then repeat with the remaining tortillas. Season with salt and allow to cool.

3. Mix the dressing ingredients together in a small bowl.

4. Very finely slice the tuna into pieces 5mm (¼ inch) thick and lay on a serving platter. Cut the apple into thin matchsticks, then add to the platter.

5. Spoon over the dressing, followed by the crispy shallots, peanuts, sliced green chilli and coriander leaves.

6. Serve to the table with a bowl of the tortillas and let people top their tortillas with a piece of tuna and a mound of the toppings!

SALMON POKE BOWL

Only make this if you can get sushi-grade salmon, as it's served raw here. People can be afraid of fish skin, but like chicken skin, you can crisp it up in the oven and turn it into a crunchy sea-flavoured garnish, taking inspiration from the Japanese condiment furikake, which is normally made with toasted seaweeds. At the same time, you can feel good about yourself for maximizing every bit of the fish.

....

Serves 2

150g (5½oz) sticky rice, sushi rice or jasmine rice

1 tablespoon white sesame seeds

2 tablespoons soy sauce

2 tablespoons rice vinegar

2 tablespoons chilli sauce, such as sriracha

1 tablespoon sesame oil

2 sushi-grade skin-on salmon fillets, skin removed and reserved

3 spring onions, green parts only, finely sliced

For the crispy salmon skin

skin from the salmon fillets (see above)

1 teaspoon shichimi togarashi (or alternatively mix together ½ teaspoon chilli flakes, 1 teaspoon white sesame seeds and a pinch of flaky sea salt)

flaky sea salt

For the mango salad

1 ripe mango, peeled, stoned and cut into 2-cm (1-inch) cubes

1 red chilli, deseeded and finely sliced

finely grated zest and juice of 1 lime

1. Start by cooking your rice according to the packet instructions, then set aside and keep warm.

2. Meanwhile, make the crispy salmon skin. Preheat the oven to 210°C (190°C fan, 410°F), Gas Mark 6½. Line a baking tray with nonstick paper.

3. Ensure all the salmon flesh has been scraped off the skin, then lay it flat on the lined tray and season generously with flaky sea salt. Place another sheet of baking paper over the skin and press down so that the skin is completely flat. Top with another baking tray, then bake for 10–15 minutes until the skin is crisp.

4. While the salmon skin is in the oven, toast the sesame seeds in a small dry frying pan over a medium heat for about 2 minutes until lightly golden. Remove from the pan and set aside to cool.

5. Remove the salmon skin from the oven and break it into small pieces, then toss with the shichimi togarashi (or chilli flakes, sesame seeds and salt).

6. Mix together the soy sauce, vinegar, chilli sauce, sesame oil and toasted sesame seeds in a bowl. Cut the salmon into 1-cm (½-inch) cubes and add to the bowl with the spring onion greens, then cover and marinate in the fridge for at least 30 minutes.

7. Toss the mango salad ingredients together in a bowl.

8. Either serve the different components in separate bowls or spoon some warm rice into serving bowls and top with the salmon and mango salad and garnish with the crispy salmon skin.

SCALLOPS WITH SALSA ROJA & BURNT CORN

This dish works perfectly as a starter, or it could be served as a main with rice or tacos. It's a fun way to use scallops, which are usually served with richer ingredients like buttery peas, black pudding or bacon. It would also be great with a ceviche of thinly sliced scallop that's just hit with lime zest and juice and salt for a lighter version.

....

Serves 4

2 cooked corn on the cob
(or use 1 small tin cooked
sweetcorn kernels, drained
and dried on kitchen paper)

12–16 prepared scallops

2–3 tablespoons olive oil

knob of butter

a handful of fresh coriander sprigs

juice of 1 lime, plus extra to serve

salt

extra virgin olive oil, to finish

For the salsa roja

300g (10½oz) cherry tomatoes

1 Scotch bonnet chilli

½ white onion, roughly chopped

3 teaspoons sugar

½ teaspoon salt

1 garlic clove, finely grated

1. Start by making the salsa roja. Blitz together the cherry tomatoes, Scotch bonnet, onion and sugar in a blender until mostly smooth, then season with the salt. Set aside.

2. Stand each corn cob in turn upright and slice down from the stalk end to cut off the kernels in long strips, keeping as many of the kernels together as possible.

3. Heat a large nonstick dry frying pan over a high heat, then once hot, add the corn kernels and char for 4–6 minutes, turning once so that they become dark in colour. Turn the heat off, then tip them out of the pan on to a plate to cool.

4. Pat the scallops dry with kitchen paper, then season generously with salt and allow them to sit for a few minutes. Place the pan back over a high heat and add the olive oil. Dry the scallops again with kitchen paper, place them in the hot pan, flat-side down, and cook for about 2–3 minutes until golden brown. Don't move or touch them for the first few minutes, allowing them to unstick themselves from the pan. Turn the scallops over, reduce the heat to low and cook for another minute, adding the butter to baste. You only need to get colour on one side, otherwise you will overcook the scallops.

5. Remove the scallops to a plate, leaving any juices behind in the pan. Add the blitzed tomato mixture, scraping any of the juices from the scallops into the sauce, and bubble over a high heat for 4–5 minutes. Once the sauce is ready, stir in the raw grated garlic. This addition makes a huge difference, giving the sauce body.

6. Toss the charred corn with lime juice and a pinch of salt.

7. Spoon the salsa roja on to individual plates and sit the scallops on top, followed by the corn and coriander. Finish with a little extra virgin olive oil, then serve immediately with fresh lime on the table.

SALT & PEPPER SQUID

When we were growing up, coming from a separated family, my dad's duty was to take us out for dinner once or twice a week. A creature of habit, he would bring us to the same places all the time. One of his selections was a Chinese restaurant called Yung's. They had a salt and pepper squid dish with crunchy Gem lettuce and white onion that had just kissed the pan. We'd drench it in soy sauce and thoroughly enjoy it. I'm sure it wasn't as good as I remember it, but it has nostalgic value. I credit these experiences with establishing my love of food, whether my dad knew that or not, and this recipe has been influenced by that dish and memory.

Serves 2

5 tablespoons vegetable or sunflower oil

2–3 long red and yellow chillies, roughly sliced

180g (6¼oz) squid, sliced into rings

3 spring onions, cut into 3-cm (1¼-inch) lengths

½ onion, cut into chunky strips

3 celery sticks, sliced 2cm (¾ inch) thick

1 tablespoon soy sauce

1 teaspoon black vinegar

salt

1. Heat 3 tablespoons of the oil in a large frying pan or wok over a medium heat. Once hot, add the chillies and fry, stirring regularly, for 5 minutes until the chillies are slightly frazzled but not coloured. Remove from the pan, season with salt and set aside to cool.

2. Pat the squid rings dry with kitchen paper. Heat the remaining oil in the same pan or wok over a high heat. When hot, add the squid and fry for 2 minutes, moving them once or twice only to ensure they take some charring.

3. Add the spring onions, onion, celery and soy sauce to the pan, and stir-fry for 1–2 minutes. Remove from the heat, then stir in the black vinegar.

4. Tip on to serving plates or a large platter, and top with the frazzled chillies.

VIETNAMESE-STYLE SEA BASS

This is probably my death row meal. I love eating a whole fish with rice. The process of 'steaming' the fish in a parcel in the oven as in this recipe allows the aromatic stuffing to really flavour the fish, but the warm salad steals the show here; the aubergine and pak choi are sautéed in shallot oil, then tossed with fresh tomatoes and dressed in the Vietnamese-inspired *nước chấm*. Feel free to skip the crispy shallots to make this recipe more seamless (which it is in any case!), as there is so much going on with the dressing already.

....

Serves 2

1 whole sea bass, cleaned and descaled

1 lemon grass stalk, halved lengthways

2-cm (¾-inch) piece of fresh root ginger, sliced into rounds

½ red chilli, cut into 3 pieces

1 quantity Crispy Shallots, using 3 shallots, oil reserved (see page 196), or 6 tablespoons vegetable or sunflower oil

salt

steamed jasmine rice, to serve

For the dressing

4 tablespoons fish sauce

finely grated zest and juice of 2 limes

2 garlic cloves, finely grated

1–2 bird's-eye chillies, finely chopped

1 shallot, finely chopped

1 teaspoon palm sugar or granulated sugar

For the vegetables

1 aubergine, cut into 2-cm (¾-inch) chunks

2 pak choi, cut into 2cm (¾-inch) pieces

100g (3½oz) cherry tomatoes, halved

For the herb salad

a handful of fresh coriander, basil and mint leaves (about 15g/½oz of each)

juice of ½ lime

1. Prepare your fish by scoring the skin in diagonal slashes a few times on both sides, then season inside and out with salt.

2. Stuff the fish cavity with the lemon grass, ginger, chilli, coriander and basil until it's full with all the flavourings, then place on a baking tray and set aside in the fridge for 30 minutes.

3. Meanwhile, mix all the dressing ingredients in a bowl.

4. Preheat the oven to 210°C (190°C fan, 410°F), Gas Mark 6½.

5. Place the stuffed fish on a large piece of nonstick baking paper or foil, then fold it up and scrunch the top so that the fish is completely sealed inside. Place the parcel on a baking tray and bake in the oven for 20–25 minutes (the cooking time may differ depending on the size of fish). You are looking for the flesh to come away from the bone effortlessly.

6. While the fish is in the oven, add 6 tablespoons of the reserved crispy shallot oil , or vegetable or sunflower oil to a large frying pan over a medium heat. Once hot, add the aubergine and sauté for 8 minutes, turning a few times, until lightly golden and soft all the way through. Now nestle the pak choi pieces into the aubergine and cook for 4 minutes until wilted and soft. Turn off the heat, then add the cherry tomatoes and the dressing.

7. Toss the herbs with the lime juice and a pinch of salt in a bowl.

8. Spoon the vegetables on to a serving plate or platter, then carefully lift the fish out of its parcel and place on top. Sprinkle over the crispy shallots, if using, then serve to the table with the dressed herbs and a bowl of steamed jasmine rice.

DRESSINGS, CRISPY THINGS & PICKLES

CRUNCHES

Crispy things that make other things better.

....

FRIED PEANUTS & CRISPY LIME LEAVES

Makes about 150g (5½oz) or enough for 4 servings

4 tablespoons vegetable oil

150g (5½oz) raw skin-on peanuts

15 fresh lime leaves

pinch of flaky sea salt

¼ teaspoon cayenne pepper

1. Set a sieve over a heatproof bowl and line a plate with kitchen paper. Heat the vegetable oil in a wok or large, deep frying pan over a high heat, then once hot, add the peanuts and toss in the oil. Let the peanuts bubble in the oil for 3–4 minutes until the skins turn red and the insides are toasted (be careful not to overdo the frying, as the peanuts will taste bitter). Add the lime leaves at the last minute to pop and crisp up in the oil. Pour the peanuts and lime leaves with their cooking oil into the sieve to drain and catch the oil, then transfer to the paper-lined plate to mop up any remaining oil. Season with the sea salt and cayenne pepper. Once cool, store in an airtight container for up to a month.

CRISPY SHALLOTS

Makes about 50g (1¾oz) or enough for 4 servings

3–6 shallots

about 100ml (3½fl oz) neutral oil, such as vegetable or sunflower oil

good pinch of salt

1. Set a sieve over a heatproof bowl and line a plate with kitchen paper. Peel and finely slice the shallots into rounds, making them as thin and even as you can – use a mandolin if you have one.

2. Add the shallots to a saucepan or wok and pour over enough oil to cover, then place over a medium-high heat and fry, stirring often so that they cook evenly, for about 6–10 minutes until they are lightly golden (keep an eye on them, as once they start to turn golden, they will go dark very fast). Pour the oil and shallots into the sieve so that the bowl underneath catches the oil. Transfer to the paper-lined plate and add the salt, then set aside to cool, reserving the flavoured oil for later use.

MAPLE SPICED PUMPKIN SEEDS

Makes about 100g (3½oz) or enough for 4 servings

4 tablespoons pumpkin seeds

1 teaspoon fennel seeds

1 teaspoon cumin seeds

1 teaspoon coriander seeds

1 teaspoon chilli powder

1 tablespoon maple syrup

1 tablespoon olive oil

½ teaspoon pul biber (Aleppo chilli flakes)

flaky sea salt

1. Preheat the oven to 200°C (180°C fan, 400°F), Gas Mark 6. Line a baking tray with nonstick baking paper.

2. Mix all the ingredients except the pul biber and salt together in a bowl. Tip on to the lined tray, spread out into an even layer and roast for 5–10 minutes until richly toasted and bubbling. Remove from the oven and set aside to cool, then satisfyingly break up with your hands and season with the pul biber and flaky sea salt. These will keep in an airtight container for up to 2 weeks.

DRESSINGS

Our salad dressings which we love so much, we've used them multiple times throughout this book.

FRENCH DRESSING

**Makes about 100ml (3½fl oz)
or enough for 4 servings**

3 tablespoons good-quality extra virgin olive oil

juice of ½ lemon

1 tablespoon white wine vinegar

½ tablespoon maple syrup

1 teaspoon English mustard

1 teaspoon wholegrain mustard

salt and freshly ground black pepper

1. In our restaurants, we blend all the ingredients together with a hand blender to get a thoroughly emulsified dressing, but if I'm at home, I just add them to a small bowl and whisk with a fork or put them in a jam jar, screw on the lid and give it a good shake until well combined and smooth.

SICHUAN PEPPERCORN DRESSING

**Makes about 150ml (5fl oz)
or enough for 4 servings**

2 tablespoons Sichuan peppercorns

½ teaspoon freshly ground black pepper

1 teaspoon chilli powder

3 tablespoons rice vinegar

3 tablespoons sunflower oil

2 tablespoons mirin

2 tablespoons soy sauce

1 tablespoon maple syrup

2 garlic cloves, finely grated

2-cm (¾-inch) piece of fresh root ginger, very finely chopped

1. Toast the Sichuan peppercorns in a small dry frying pan over a medium heat for about 2 minutes, or until they start to smoke and you can smell their aromatics. Remove from the pan and set aside to cool slightly.

2. Roughly crush the toasted Sichuan peppercorns using a pestle and mortar or blender until you have a coarse powder. Add to a small bowl with all the remaining ingredients and whisk together with a fork.

BASIL CAESAR DRESSING

**Makes about 150ml (5fl oz)
or enough for 4 servings**

large handful of basil (about 20g/¾oz)

4 anchovy fillets in oil

2 small garlic cloves, peeled

2 heaped tablespoons grated Parmesan cheese

1 egg yolk

juice of ½ lemon

1 tablespoon white wine vinegar

1 tablespoon water

1 teaspoon English mustard

100ml (3½fl oz) olive oil

salt and freshly ground black pepper

1. Blitz together all the ingredients except the olive oil and seasoning in a small bowl with a hand blender or in a blender until smooth. Then, with the blender running, very slowly add the oil until you have a smooth and creamy dressing. Season to taste with salt and pepper.

CRISPY CHILLI OIL

**Makes enough to fill a standard
454g (1lb) jam jar**

8 garlic cloves

6 banana shallots

350ml (12fl oz) sunflower oil

70g (2½oz) raw skin-on peanuts

1 teaspoon fennel seeds

2 tablespoons sesame seeds

1 teaspoon sugar

large pinch of flaky sea salt

1 teaspoon chicken stock powder
(optional)

2 tablespoons Korean chilli flakes
(add more if you want more spice)

2–3 whole dried red chillies (use
as many or as few as you want),
roughly chopped

3-cm (1¼-inch) piece of fresh root
ginger, peeled and roughly sliced

2 tablespoons Sichuan peppercorns

2 star anise

1 cinnamon stick

1 teaspoon black vinegar (optional)

salt

1. Peel and very thinly slice the
garlic and shallots so that the
slices are all even in size, using
a mandolin if you have one.

2. Set a sieve over a heatproof
bowl. Pour the sunflower oil
into a saucepan, then add the
shallots with a pinch of salt to
the cold oil and place over a
medium-high heat. Allow the
oil to heat up with the shallots
in it, then fry for 4–5 minutes,
stirring every so often so that
they cook evenly.

3. Add the garlic, peanuts and
fennel seeds and continue to
cook for a further 2–3 minutes
until they are all lightly golden.
Keep an eye on them here, as
once the garlic starts to turn
golden, it will quickly burn.
Pour the oil and aromatics
into the sieve so that the bowl
underneath catches the oil.
We'll use this oil, so don't
throw it away!

4. Add the sesame seeds, sugar,
flaky sea salt, the chicken
stock powder, if using, the
chilli flakes and chopped dried
chillies to a heatproof bowl.

5. Pour the strained oil back into
the pan and add the ginger,
Sichuan peppercorns, star
anise and cinnamon. Simmer
for about 2 minutes, then turn
off the heat and allow to infuse
for 2 minutes. Now pour the oil
over the sesame seed and chilli
mixture in the bowl and finally
stir in the shallots, garlic,
peanuts and fennel seeds.
Allow to cool completely, then
taste for seasoning. You can
add a little black vinegar here
if you have some. Once cooled,
transfer it to a sterilized
airtight jar. It will keep for
2–3 months in a cool, dry place.

PAPRIKA YOGURT

**Makes about 250g (9oz)
or enough for 4 servings**

6 tablespoons natural yogurt

1 tablespoon mayonnaise

3 garlic cloves, very finely chopped

1 teaspoon sweet paprika

1 teaspoon smoked paprika

1 teaspoon harissa

juice of ½ lemon

juice of ½ lime

handful of finely chopped chives

1. Mix all the ingredients
together in a bowl.

MISO MAPLE MARINADE
& DRESSING

**Makes about 225ml (8fl oz)
or enough for 4 servings**

3 tablespoons sunflower oil

3 tablespoons maple syrup

2 tablespoons white miso paste

2 tablespoons soy sauce

2 tablespoons rice vinegar, plus
1 tablespoon if using as a dressing

1. Mix all the ingredients
together in a small bowl until
smooth and creamy. This will
keep in the fridge for up to
3 months.

THINGS WE LIKE TO PICKLE

I'm not one for overcomplicating pickles with seasonings and spices, so I just use good seasonal fresh vegetables, a well-balanced pickling liquor and a simple process. You can eat the pickles on the day of making, but for best results store in the fridge for 24–72 hours before eating. Most of the pickles here should last for at least a month in the fridge, except where we have noted otherwise.

MASTER PICKLE LIQUOR

225ml (8fl oz) boiling water

125ml (4fl oz) rice vinegar

6 tablespoons sugar

2¼ teaspoons flaky sea salt

Stir together the boiling water, vinegar, sugar and salt in a medium heatproof bowl, then give it a good whisk until the sugar and salt have dissolved. Leave to cool (unless you are pickling red cabbage – see below), then add the vegetables you are pickling and make sure they are fully submerged. Transfer to a sterilized container if storing in the fridge for later use.

SMALL BATCH MASTER QUICK PICKLE LIQUOR

You can make a small batch of quick pickle using any of the vegetables opposite – just use this reduced pickle liquor recipe and make sure however much veg you are pickling is fully submerged in the liquor.

3 tablespoons rice vinegar

1 tablespoon sugar

¼ teaspoon flaky sea salt

3 tablespoons boiling water

Add the vinegar, sugar and salt to a small bowl, pour over the boiling water and stir until the sugar has dissolved.

PICKLED RED CABBAGE

Finely shred ½ red cabbage, add to the master pickle liquor while it's still warm (this allows it to flavour the cabbage more quickly) and scrunch it a little with your hands so that it's well coated in the liquid. After 10 minutes, the cabbage will start to turn bright pink. Serve straight away.

PICKLED CARROTS & BEAN SPROUTS

Peel 2 carrots, then slice into long, thin matchsticks, or use a julienne peeler if you have one. Wash a large handful of bean sprouts and drain. Add to the cooled master pickle liquor and scrunch a little with your hands so that the vegetables are well coated. Serve straight away.

PICKLED DAIKON & CARROTS

Prepare as for the pickled carrots & bean sprouts opposite, but replace the bean sprouts with a 10-cm (4-inch) piece of daikon, peeled and sliced into long, thin matchsticks.

PICKLED CELERY & CARROTS

Veg that cook together pickle together! Peel 3 celery sticks to remove the strings, then cut into half-moons 1cm (½ inch) thick. Peel 3 carrots, then cut in half lengthways and slice into half-moons of a similar size. Add the veg to the cooled master pickle liquor so that they are completely submerged.

PICKLED BIRD'S-EYE CHILLIES

I always have bird's-eye chillies pickling in my fridge, as they are so spicy that it takes a while for me to work through them. Wash the chillies before using, then remove the stalks with a sharp knife. Place in a sterilized airtight jar, pour over enough of the cooled master pickle liquor to submerge and seal with the lid. These will last indefinitely in your fridge.

PICKLED SHALLOTS & CHILLIES

Peel and slice 3 shallots along with 3 green chillies and 3 red chillies into even rounds and add to the cooled master pickle liquor.

PICKLED CUCUMBER

Cut 1 whole cucumber into rounds 1cm (½ inch) thick and add to the cooled master pickle liquor for a fresh, crunchy pickle.

PINK ONIONS

Peel 3 red onions, cut in half and slice into half-moons, then add to the cooled master pickle liquor. They are ready to eat right away but will turn bright pink if stored overnight in an airtight container in the fridge.

INDEX Main recipes are indicated in **bold**

marinades
  curried mayonnaise 158
  garlic & herb 133
  ginger & chilli 115
  harissa 164
  miso maple 102, 114, 176, **199**
mayonnaise
  basil Caesar dressing **197**
  garlic 118, 172
  prawn cocktail sauce 183
meatballs
  lamb 160–1
  pork 140–1
mint dressing 17
mirin & soy dressing 36
miso maple marinade 102, 114, 176, **199**
miso maple salad dressing 22–3
miso paste 109
mozzarella, in pasta salad 123
mushrooms, miso shrooms 113–14
mustard 10, 18

N

nam pla prik dressing 146, 153
noodles
  cashew, Thai-style 170–1
  cold kimchi noodles 106–7
  flat rice, chicken pho ga 139
  pickled, with miso trout 176
  rice, with pork meatballs 140
  udon, gochugang bowl 115

O

oils 10
  chilli 43, 72, 145, **199**
onions
  caramelized 127
  griddle-cooked 153
  miso maple 94–5
onions, red
  'jammy' red pepper salad 20–1
  orange & burrata salad 61
  quick-pickled 123, 161, **201**
  tomato & bread salad 50

orange
  blood orange honey 98
  & burrata salad 60–1
  & chilli dressing 134
  fennel & kohlrabi salad 30
orzo, basil, red peppers & pine nuts 120–1
oyster sauce 87, 109, 153

P

pak choi 192
paprika salt 71
paprika yogurt 133, **199**
pasta, summer pasta salad 122–3
peanut butter 137
peanuts
  crispy chilli oil 199
  fried 27, 83, 110, 142, **196**
  roasted salted 40, 140, 176, 184
  & sesame brittle **114**, 137
  spicy 127
peas, in salsa verde 46–7
pecorino cheese 76
peppers, piquillo 48–9
peppers, red
  basil orzo & pine nuts 120–1
  sweet 'jammy' salad 20–1
  Thai-style noodles 171
  & tofu, with pine nuts 36–7
pesto, walnut 79
pickled vegetables 10
  bean sprouts 113, **201**
  carrots 113, 149, 176, **201**
  celery & carrot 149
  chilli 84, 91
  courgette 45
  cucumber 29, 137, **201**
  daikon 176, **201**
  master pickle liquor **200**
  quick-pickled 123, 161, **200**
  red cabbage 23, 115, 164
  red onions 123, 161
  salsa 149
  shallot 29, 91, 137
  sour grapes 56

pine nuts 36, 120
pistachio 45, 49
plums, sweet & sour 58–9
poke bowl, salmon 186–7
pomegranate 128, 161
pork
  laab with red curry magic dust 146–7
  Vietnamese-style meatballs & rice noodles 140–1
potatoes
  chaat, with tamarind yogurt 84–5
  potato tartare 38–9
prawns 170–1, 182–3
preserved vegetables 10
pul biber 17, 24
pumpkin seeds 55, 164, **196**

R

radishes 142
ratatouille con tomate 88–9
remoulade, celeriac 154
rice
  coriander & spring onion 137
  green coconut 124–5
  paprika chica 132–3
  salmon poke bowl 187
  toasted, red curry 146
  Tutt's 'crispy' pilau 126–7
  Vietnamese-style sea bass 192–3
ricotta cheese 45, 46, 56
rocket 20–1, 118, 120
romesco 71

S

salmon 176, 186–7
salsa
  hazelnut & avocado 183
  parsley & caper 162
  pickled 149
  roja 188
  salsa verde 46–7, 161
  spring onion 65
  sun-dried tomato 80

GLOSSARY

UK	US
aubergine	eggplant
baking paper	parchment paper
baking tray	baking sheet
beef tomato	beefsteak tomato
beetroot	beets
bird's-eye chilli	Thai chili
butter beans	lima beans
Butterhead lettuce	Butter lettuce
caster sugar	superfine sugar
cavolo nero	Tuscan kale
chickpeas	garbanzo beans
chicory	Belgian endive
chilli flakes	red pepper flakes
clingfilm	plastic wrap
coriander	cilantro
corn on the cob	ears of corn
cornflour	cornstarch
Cos lettuce	Romaine lettuce
courgette	zucchini
fish fingers	fish sticks
flaked almonds	slivered almonds
frying pan	skillet
grill	broiler
king prawns	jumbo shrimp
kitchen paper	paper towels
Little Gem lettuce	substitute Baby Romaine lettuce or Romaine hearts
natural yogurt	plain yogurt
pak choi	bok choy
red pepper	bell pepper
pickled gherkins	dill pickles
rocket	arugula
self-raising flour	self-rising flour
sirloin steak	strip or striploin steak
spring onions	scallions
starter	appetizer
stock powder/cube	bouillon powder/cube
sweetheart/hispi cabbage	conehead cabbage
tea towel	dish towel
Tenderstem broccoli	broccolini

ACKNOWLEDGEMENTS

The truth is this book would not be possible without the help of many people.

First, our team at Sprout. Too many to name, but every one of our chefs, managers, front of house, kitchen porters, farmers, operators, finance team, marketers and food developers. Without your daily dedication, passion and hard work this book would not exist. You are what make our business special, so a big thank you!

A special thanks to our mum for always supporting and encouraging us, especially when it came to being adventurous with food. We love you mum!

Thank you, Rosaleen Blair, for giving us the use of your home to shoot this book. My apartment could not have handled the amount we had to cook. We love you, too!

To our cousin Tom Kelly, who initially came up with the name 'Sprout' many years ago, and 'Saladology' for this book, there is no greater guy to bounce an idea off. Thanks TK!

To Kitty Coles, who has been my support from day one of recipe testing, right until the end. Thank you for your commitment, your style and for being my friend.

To Matt Russell, our photographer who captured the food so beautifully, and Alana Margaruite McCarthy for assisting throughout the shoot with such positivity.

We are incredibly grateful to Alison Starling and all the team at Octopus for trusting us with this project. Special thanks to Jonathan Christie for his design work and multiple video calls, and Sybella Stephens for editing my writing into something that makes sense.

A special mention to our partner on the Sprout Farm – Gar, or Gung Ho, Whelan as Jack likes to call him. Thanks for helping make our farm dreams a reality.

To all our backers, mentors and our board for their continued support – thank you.

Lastly, an acknowledgement to the amazing restaurateurs, chefs, cookbook writers and teachers who have inspired me with their creativity, passion, experiences, methods and ideas. Thanks x

About the author

Theo Kirwan and his brother Jack are the co-founders of Sprout & Co. With restaurants in and around Dublin, Sprout is the leading brand in Ireland for local, seasonal and flavourful food. In 2018 the brothers started their own organic farm in County Kildare, cutting their supply chain from farm to restaurant to just 24 hours. Theo, a former actor and graduate of the Ballymaloe cookery school, has led Sprout & Co's online presence with his recipe videos, gaining a loyal following of people who get just as excited about food as he does.

First published in Great Britain in 2024
by Mitchell Beazley, an imprint of
Octopus Publishing Group Ltd
Carmelite House, 50 Victoria Embankment,
London EC4Y 0DZ
www.octopusbooks.co.uk

An Hachette UK Company
www.hachette.co.uk

Distributed in the US by Hachette Book Group
1290 Avenue of the Americas, 4th and 5th Floors, New York, NY 10104

Distributed in Canada by Canadian Manda Group
664 Annette St., Toronto, Ontario, Canada M6S 2C8

ISBN 978 1 78472 915 8

A CIP catalogue record for this book is available from the British Library.

Printed and bound in China

10 9 8 7 6 5 4 3 2 1

Photographer: Matt Russell
Front Cover Photography: Dora Kazmierak
Food & Props Stylist: Kitty Coles

Publisher: Alison Starling
Creative Director: Jonathan Christie
Senior Managing Editor: Sybella Stephens
Copy Editor: Jo Richardson
Assistant Production Manager: Emily Noto